Battle of Cowpens:
Primary & Contemporary Accounts

EDITED BY ANDREW WATERS

Copyright © 2019 Andrew Waters

Cover image: Col. (William) Washington at the Battle of Cowpens, artist unknown. Courtesy of Library of Congress.

All collected material is from the public domain.

All rights reserved.

ISBN-13: 978-0-578-50624-1

For Anne & Eli

CONTENTS

	Introduction: The American Revolution's Unlikely Turning Point by Andrew Waters	7
1	Correspondence Between Nathanael Greene, Daniel Morgan, and Otho Holland Williams	25
2	Correspondence Between Banastre Tarleton and Charles, Lord Cornwallis	38
3	From *A Journal of the Southern Expedition* by William Seymour	45
4	James Simon to William Washington	51
5	From *The Memoir of Major Thomas Young*	54
6	From *Autobiography of a Revolutionary Soldier* by James P. Collins	62
7	Samuel Hammond's "Notes" on the Battle of Cowpens	65
8	From *A History of the Campaigns of 1780 and 1781* by Banastre Tarleton	69
9	From *Strictures on Lt. Col. Tarleton's History "of the Campaigns of 1780 and 1781"* by Roderick Mackenzie	81
10	Daniel Morgan's Report on the Battle of Cowpens	93
11	From *The Account of Charles, Lord Cornwallis, to Henry Clinton*	98
12	From *Memoirs of the War in the Southern Department of the United States* by Henry Lee	102

13	From *The History of the Origin, Progress and Termination of the American War* by Charles Stedman	112
14	From *The History of South Carolina, From a British Province to an Independent State* by David Ramsay, M.D.	120
15	Congressional Proclamation and Related Correspondence	128
	About the Editor	133

INTRODUCTION

COWPENS: THE AMERICAN REVOLUTION'S UNLIKELY TURNING POINT
By ANDREW WATERS

Cowpens seems an unlikely hinge for the American Revolution. Far, far from Boston Harbor or Philadelphia's Independence Hall, the solemn encampment of Valley Forge, or the sweeping coastal views of Yorktown, it was a literal cow pasture, a place where local farmers collected their herds before driving them to market, located at the far reaches of what was then the South Carolina frontier. Yet, most historians of the time, along with many of today, agree the war did hinge at Cowpens during the battle there on January 17, 1781, when General Daniel Morgan and his mixed force of Continental soldiers and Patriot militia miraculously defeated a superior British force under the command of Lieutenant-colonel Banastre Tarleton.

"Tarleton's defeat was the first link, in a grand chain of causes, which finally drew down ruin, both in North and South Carolina, on the royal interest," writes David Ramsay, one of the American Revolution's earliest historians, not a witness to

Cowpens but one who was in South Carolina at the time. And Charles Stedman, a British Army officer under Charles Cornwallis during the Southern Campaign, states even more definitively, "The defeat of his majesty's troops at the Cowpens formed a very principal link in the chain of circumstances which led to the independence of America."[i] Referencing the Battle of Bennington on August 16, 1777, a part of the Saratoga campaign that resulted in the surrender of the British Army under General John Burgoyne, the estimable Henry "Light Horse Harry" Lee, wrote, "The victory of Cowpens was to the South what that of Bennington had been to the North."

Modern historians agree. "The victory (at Cowpens) was a 'Great Thing Indeed,'" writes John Buchanan in the *Road to Guilford Courthouse*, his seminal work about the Southern Campaign. "Its primary consequence was the loss to Cornwallis of his light troops, which would have a crucial effect on the balance of the campaign. Its secondary consequence was psychological. Morale soared."[ii] And Mark M. Boatner, the author of the classic *Encyclopedia of the American Revolution*, provides this summary, "Although the Battle of Cowpens saved half of Greene's army and destroyed a large part of Cornwallis's—depriving him of light troops when he needed them most—its farther reaching effects were to raise patriot morale when it badly needed raising. Southern militia started turning out in greater numbers, and the North started sending the support the South so badly needed. The substantial but not fatal British tactical reverse at Cowpens led Cornwallis into strategic errors that *were* fatal to the British at Yorktown."[iii]

The origin of this unlikely victory began with what was itself an unlikely strategic gambit: General Nathanael Greene's decision to split his light troops under Morgan from his main army and send them into western South Carolina. "You are appointed to the command of a corps of Light Infantry, a detachment of Militia, and Lt. Col. Washington's Regiment of Light Dragoons," Greene commanded Morgan on December 16, 1780. "With these troops you will proceed to the West side of the

Catawba river, where you will be joined by a body of Volunteer Militia."

Greene's decision was born out of his small army's desperate situation, though it was not without its tactical considerations. Upon arriving in Charlotte to assume command of the Southern Army from Horatio Gates, Greene wrote to George Washington, complaining: "Nothing can be more wretched and distressing than the condition of the troops, starving with cold and hunger, without tents and camp equipage."[iv]

His strategy was to send his light troops under Morgan west of the Catawba River to the western reaches of South Carolina, where they were "to give protection to that part of the country and spirit up the people—to annoy the enemy in that quarter—collect the provisions and forage out of the way of the enemy, which you will have formed into a number of small magazines, in or near the position you may think proper to take." Meanwhile, Greene would take the main body of the army to a "camp of repose" at the Cheraws on the PeeDee river in South Carolina, where he hoped for more abundant provisions and the opportunity to instill a sense of discipline into his ragtag troops.

In truth, it was a strategy Greene formulated long before he arrived in Charlotte. He had proposed use of a "Flying Army," a select force of light infantry and mounted troops operating separate from the main army, to both Washington and Alexander Hamilton after receiving command of the Southern Army in early November.[v]

The decision was a monumental one, leading to the conflict at Cowpens and the demise of Cornwallis, as our historians have already pronounced, though it defied the military convention against splitting an inferior army in the face of a superior foe. Subsequently, it has fascinated historians for centuries, who occasionally reference it as illustration of Greene's unconventional brilliance, even describing it "as the most audacious and ingenious piece of military strategy of the war."[vi]

But such a split was hardly novel to the American Revolution. Both sides had employed the tactic in the northeastern theater, most famously, Washington splitting his Army at New York and Long Island in August 1776. Even the case of Patrick Ferguson and his Loyalist division operating semi-independently of Cornwallis in the campaign that also ended disastrously at King's Mountain might serve as an example, though the maxim proved true in both instances.

The novelty of Greene's strategy was the great distance between the two Continental corps, well over a hundred miles, increasing their peril. Attempting to mitigate this danger, Greene would permit Morgan to operate "either offensively or defensively as your own prudence and discretion may direct," but he urged Morgan to act "with caution . . . avoiding surprizes by every possible precaution."[vii]

Though born from necessity, the move was not without its strategic advantages. The great distance between Morgan and Greene placed Cornwallis in a quandary. If he moved west to engage Morgan, he left open his eastern flank, exposing Charleston to Greene. If he moved east toward Greene, he imperiled his western outposts. As Greene later explained, "It [the split] makes the most of my inferior force, for it compels my adversary to divide his, and holds him in doubt as to his own line of conduct. He cannot leave Morgan behind him to come at me, or his posts of Ninety-Six and Augusta would be exposed. And he cannot chase Morgan far, or prosecute his views upon Virginia, while I am here with the whole open country before me. I am as near to Charleston, as he is."[viii]

Cornwallis was perplexed by Greene's movements, refusing to believe initial reports[ix] then disregarding them as ineffectual. Even if he recognized the threat to Charleston and the British garrison at Georgetown, "from every thing I hear of his force I do not think it possible for him to strike any blow that would materially affect my movements."[x] And Cornwallis had an ace up his sleeve: Major General Alexander Leslie arrived in Charleston with 1,500 British reinforcements on December 14.[xi] According to Tarleton's memoir, Cornwallis believed any offensive operations contemplated by Greene in the east would soon be disregarded by news of Leslie's arrival.[xii] Therefore, Cornwallis saw no reason not to move forward with his planned invasion of North Carolina. But first he had to await Leslie's march from Charleston to the South Carolina interior.

Greene was not aware of Leslie's arrival when he made his decision, learning of it only on December 24 in a letter from Francis Marion.[xiii] Though he had been tracking Leslie's movements through his correspondents, he believed it bound for the Cape Fear region around Wilmington, not Charleston. But the development mattered little to his plan, for his objectives were not offensive. Even the great Nathanael Greene could not foresee the momentous happenstance his strategies would conceive.

***

As momentous as was Greene's decision to split his forces, more remarkable still was the man he placed in charge of his "Flying Army," the legendary Daniel Morgan. Born in 1736 to an ironmaster in Bucks County, Pennsylvania, Morgan left home at the age of seventeen, exploring the Virginia frontier, working as a miller and teamster, learning the manners and customs of a backwoodsman. He was imposing in physical appearance, well over six feet, stout and muscular but athletic. Though his temper could flare, Morgan's benevolent nature and good humor, along with a keen instinct for human nature, drew men to him. By the time of the conflict known as the "French and Indian War," he had established his own business as a teamster, and in 1755 he joined British General Edward Braddock's expedition against the French in that capacity, traveling with Braddock's Army to fight in what is now the area of Pittsburgh, Pennsylvania. During this service, he struck an English officer who had hit him with the flat of his sword and received a punishment of five hundred lashes for his insubordination. Later in life he would often joke that the English drummer miscounted, and he owed the British one "stripe." By 1762 the six-foot, two-hundred-pound Morgan had left British service and settled near Winchester, Virginia, prospering as a farmer but returning to English service in the Indian conflicts known as Pontiac's War and Dunmore's War.

"His courage, daring, and resourcefulness in military affairs, added to his other characteristics, made him a great leader of men in the war upon which he was now entering."[xiv] In 1775 he was commissioned captain of a Viriginia rifle company and assimilated into the Continental Army during the siege of Boston. When Benedict Arnold was wounded during the assault on Quebec, December 31, 1775, Morgan took command but was taken prisoner during the battle and not exchanged until the fall of 1776. Later that fall, he was commissioned a colonel and the next year he served valiantly with Gates during the Saratoga Campaign.

After Saratoga, Morgan refused to join in Gates's intrigues against Washington and returned to the main body of the Army, wintering at Valley Forge. In 1779 he resigned from the Army in a dispute over a promotion, though he claimed bad health, and returned to his farm near Winchester, but in June 1780, Congress ordered him to report to Gates once more in the Southern Theater. A promotion did not accompany the orders, and Morgan delayed, but after the disaster at Camden he relented, taking command of Gates's light troops on October 2, just a few days after arriving in the southern camp. He would retain command of the light troops under Greene. On October 13, Congress granted him the commission of brigadier general he had long sought.[xv]

By the winter of 1780-1781, Morgan's long years of campaigning had taken a toll. The "sciatica"—probably a combination of a slipped disk, hemorrhoids, and rheumatism[xvi]—was exacerbated by long hours in the saddle and several weeks of heavy rain. "The damp ground of the camp and the frequent soaking from the incessant rains brought on so great an aching in his bones and a stiffening in his joints that already he found it all but impossible to crawl aboard a horse," characterizes one writer.[xvii]

Clearly, Morgan was more than a little cranky during his trip west. Writing to Greene from his camp on the Pacolet River, at a place called Grindal Shoals, to the south of what is now Spartanburg, South Carolina, Morgan complained about the scarcity of food and forage: "I find it impracticable to procure more provisions in this quarter than is absolutely necessary for our own immediate consumption, indeed it has been with the greatest difficulty that we have been able to effect this."[xviii] The local militia he was supposed to "spirit up" were a big part of his problem. Their horses denuded the countryside of every strand of grass and grain in the surrounding countryside; their leaders could be temperamental and difficult.

But Morgan's presence was leaving its effect on Cornwallis, and after a combined force of Continental cavalry and local militia under Lieutenant-Colonel William Washington, a cousin of George Washington, defeated a force of Loyalists at a place called Hammond's Store on December 27, 1780, and then went on to capture a Loyalist outpost known as "Williams Fort," Cornwallis grew concerned about the safety of his garrison at Ninety Six, a trading post in the far western reaches of South Carolina that had become an important anchor in the British line of defense.

Against Morgan, Cornwallis dispatched Lieutenant-Colonel Banastre Tarleton, along with the majority of his own light troops. Born in 1754, just twenty-six at the time of Cowpens, Tarleton had emerged as Cornwallis's most trusted officer during the course of the Southern Campaign. Of aristocratic stock, Tarleton had entered the British Army in 1775 as a coronet, but quickly rose through the ranks. By 1778 he received a field promotion to lieutenant-colonel and placed in command of the British Legion, a "Provincial" unit comprised mostly of troops raised in America, consisting roughly of one-half light infantry and one-half mounted dragoons. Under Tarleton's command, the Legion scored several victories in the campaigning around Charleston in spring 1780, securing for their cocky commander Cornwallis's trust and faith. Most notoriously, Tarleton was in command at the Waxhaws on May 29, 1780, when his command butchered American soldiers as they attempted to surrender. From this incident arose the term "Tarleton's quarters," characterizing the brutality of the British Army in the South. "As a leader of cavalry, he was unmatched on either side for alertness and rapidity of movement, dash, daring and vigor of attack," writes Christopher Ward. "As a man, he was cold-hearted, vindictive, and utterly ruthless. He wrote his name in letters of blood all across the history of the war in the South."[xix]

As you shall read, Cornwallis and Tarleton (or Tarleton and Cornwallis, based on Tarleton's own version of the events) hatched a scheme to trap Morgan. Beginning in early January, Tarleton and his light troops would push Morgan to the north, while Cornwallis and the main body of the British Army would come up the east side of the Broad River, catching Morgan as he attempted to reunite with Greene. True, when Tarleton wrote to Cornwallis on January 4, 1781, "When I advance, I must either destroy Morgan's corps, or push it before me over Broad river, towards King's mountain. The advance of the army should commence (when your lordship orders this corps to move) onwards for King's mountain," Cornwallis responded on January 5, "You have exactly done what I wished you to do; and understood my intentions perfectly."[xx]

But clearly the wavelength of the British commander and his protégé were not as aligned as Cornwallis believed. Cornwallis wanted the push against Morgan to be the initial phase of his planned invasion of North Carolina, and for that he still needed Leslie's reinforcements, who hadn't yet joined him on their march from Charleston. Always eager for action, Tarleton either misunderstood Cornwallis's delay, or ignored it. By January 15, the tempestuous Tarleton received word

Morgan had evacuated his camp on the Pacolet River the day before. Eager to pounce on his prey, Tarleton decided he could wait no longer for a coordinated attack with Cornwallis and commenced his ill-fated advance against Morgan.

Morgan meanwhile was well-apprised of both Cornwallis and Tarleton's movements. Local militia continued to coalesce at or near Morgan's camp, and they were spoiling for a fight. Morgan didn't like his strategic position on the Pacolet and retreated north by northeast, coming to a halt at the Cowpens on the evening of January 16, a few miles south of the Broad River. The men grumbled. "We were very anxious for battle, and many a hearty curse had been vented against Gen. Morgan during that day's March, for retreating, as we thought, to avoid a fight," recalled Thomas Young, a South Carolina militia soldier who accompanied Morgan on his march.[xxi]

Whether Morgan was planning for a fight all along or only gauging the psychic vibe of his ragtag troops we will never know. We know Morgan didn't want to cross the Broad on the run from Tarleton, fearing Tarleton would attack his rear in the midst of the crossing while he was at his most vulnerable. We also know the open, rolling fields of the Cowpens formed a battlefield to his liking. Arising about three hundred yards from the southern edge of the forest from which Morgan had arrived, and from which Tarleton would pursue, was a hill, really more of a crest in the rolling landscape, and about eighty yards beyond it, a smaller hill, with more open wood behind and the Broad River a few miles in his rear. Later, historians would criticize him for his choice; the open field played to his opponent's advantage, given Tarleton's superiority in cavalry. But from long years of fighting with irregular troops, Morgan knew that cover only served as a temptation for his men to break and run in the heat of battle, and the swollen Broad River in his rear would only increase their determination to stand and fight.

But let us hear from Morgan himself, in answer to his critics:

"I would not have had a swamp in the view of my militia on any consideration; they would have made for it, and nothing could have detained them from it. And as to covering my wings, I knew my adversary, and was perfectly sure I should have nothing but downright fighting. As to retreat, it was the very thing I wished to cut off all hope of. I would have thanked Tarleton had he surrounded me with his cavalry. It would have been better than placing my own men in the rear to shoot down those who broke from the ranks. When men are forced to fight, they will sell their lives dearly . . . Had I crossed the river, one half of the militia would have immediately abandoned me."[xxii]

Militia flocked to Morgan's camp during the night of January 16, including the great South Carolina militia general Andrew Pickens with about 150 men. According to a reminiscence by Lieutenant-colonel John Eager Howard, who would go on to command the main line in the battle to come, it was not until Pickens arrived that Morgan decided to fight.[xxiii] The great general now began to lay out his battle plan: on his first line, closest to the woods from which the pursuing Tarleton would emerge, Morgan would place about 150 militia sharpshooters; about 150 yards behind them would be a line of his main militia body, about three hundred in number, under the command of Andrew Pickens. To his skirmishers he ordered them to open a scattered fire, then fall back to Pickens line. Once joined by the skirmishers, Pickens was ordered to hold his fire until the enemy was within fifty yards, then fire two rounds, focusing on the British officers. At the crest of the hill, he would place his main line of Continentals, along with militia from Georgia and Virginia on the ends of the line. This line would be commanded by John Eager Howard, the experienced Maryland lieutenant colonel. In reserve would be placed his eighty cavalry under the command of William Washington, along with a small contingent of mounted militia. Once Pickens's militia had fired their two rounds, they were to retreat in good order around the left side of Howard's main line, then re-form and hold in reserve.[xxiv]

In placing his irregular troops at the front of his formation, Morgan's disposition broke military orthodox, which demanded placing the strongest troops in front. His officers protested as much. "The profession of arms does not often attract innovative minds," noted John Buchanan. "This untutored son of the frontier [Morgan] was the only general in the American Revolution, on either side, to produce a significant original tactical thought."[xxv] And Morgan knew his men. All through the night he visited their camp fires, joking and rehashing his old anecdote about owing the British a lick, perhaps even displaying the scars from his long-ago whipping to the rapt crowd.[xxvi]

Thomas Young remembered it well: "It was upon this occasion I was more perfectly convinced of Gen.'s qualifications to command militia, than I had ever before been. He went among the volunteers, helped them fix their swords, joked with them about their sweet-hearts, told them to keep in good spirits, and the day would be ours. And long after I laid down, he was going about among the soldiers encouraging them, and telling them that the old wagoner would crack his whip over Ben. (Tarleton) in the morning, as sure as they lived. 'Just hold your heads, boys, three fires,' he would say, 'and you are free, and then when you return to your homes, how the old folks will bless you, and the girls kiss you, for your gallant conduct!' I don't believe he slept a wink that night!"[xxvii]

If such hyperbole is the ingredient of legend, then let us embrace this dish, for on the following morning of January 17, 1781, an American legend was made. Morgan knew his adversary well. Tarleton had pushed his troops through the night, hoping to catch Morgan on the run. By the time his British forces emerged from the wood shortly before seven that morning, after a hard night's ride, Morgan's men had breakfasted and were in battle position. Tarleton's men were exhausted, but Tarleton was in no mood for delay. He formed his infantry in a line, with a force of fifty dragoons on both its right and left side, and a reserve of infantry and about two hundred dragoons in the rear. Before his lines had even formed, however, he ordered their attack.

I shall not linger long here on the disposition of the British troops, or the battlefield play-by-play. Many of the accounts included in this collection detail these actions with more accuracy and force than I could ever recount, writing from the comfort of my desk, surrounded by their books and stories. But one magic moment bears recounting. After the militia had perfectly executed their orders, killing or wounding several British officers with their long rifles, they retreated according to the plan. From behind his main line of Continentals, Morgan rushed to where the militia was reforming to assist Pickens in keeping them orderly, knowing their natural inclination was to scatter. Waving his sword, Morgan cried out, cried out, "Form, form, my brave fellows! Give them one more fire and the day is ours. Old Morgan was never beaten."[xxviii]

The militia responded, and followed their leaders in a wide arc behind the Continental line toward Howard's right flank. The fighting had been going on for just over half an hour. About this time, Howard ordered his right flank to pivot in order to oppose a British flanking maneuver, but the order was misunderstood; instead, the Continentals on the far right commenced a retreat, "first a part, and then the whole of the company," Howard later remembered. "The officers along the line seeing this, and supposing that orders had been given for a retreat, faced their men about and moved off."[xxix] Seeing the retreat, Morgan detached from where he had been rallying the militia and rode to Howard, who assured him the men were still in order.

By this time many of the British infantry's officers had been wounded or killed. Observing what they believed to be an American retreat, the British soldiers instinctively commenced a charge against the Continental right flank, believing their enemy beaten, breaking their ranks to push forward. But Morgan and his officers had regained control of their own line and chosen the spot where their men would turn to face the British. At 7:45 that morning, Morgan gave the order to turn, shouting "Face about boys! Give them one good fire, and the victory is ours!" as he rode up and down the line.[xxx]

The moment of victory was at hand. The Continentals turned on command to face their pursuing enemy, who were by now perhaps as close as ten yards. With Howard's order to "fire" the Continental rifles exploded in the face of the stunned British. While the British recoiled in shock and confusion from the withering fire, Howard gave the order for his men to charge bayonets. This order was completed with "such Address that they [the British infantry] fled with utmost Precipitation, leaving the Field Pieces in our Possession. We pushed our Advantage so effectually, that they never had an Opportunity of rallying," Morgan recounted.[xxxi]

One last moment of myth. During the closing moments of the battle, Banastre Tarleton rallied about forty dragoons who had not yet either been captured or fled the field for one last charge in an attempt to recover his captured artillery. According to some accounts, William Washington ordered his cavalry to charge against Tarleton, but most of his men did not hear him, and those that did were far behind their leader. By now Tarleton's dragoons were retiring, but Tarleton himself was said to turn and encounter Washington in a swirling fight from horseback. Tarleton's point-blank pistol shot missed Washington but wounded his horse, then Tarleton wheeled and rode away. Whether or not the British officer Washington "dueled" was Tarleton has never actually been confirmed. British accounts suggest it wasn't.[xxxii] Nevertheless, the tale was widely recounted by American historians, as you shall read in the account of Henry Lee, and has become a part of our American myth.

The British defeat was complete. Their killed totaled approximately one hundred, including a large portion of their officer corps. Nearly ninety percent of the British force was either killed or captured, including about 230 wounded. In addition, the British lost their two artillery pieces, thirty-five baggage wagons, one hundred dragoon horses, a large store of ammunition, and sixty slaves. In contrast, only twelve Americans were killed and sixty wounded.[xxxiii]

"The troops I have the honor to command have gained a complete victory over a detachment from British Army commanded by Lieut.-Col. Tarleton," Morgan wrote in his report of the battle to Nathanael Greene.[xxxiv] Greene received news of the victory on January 24th. "The event is glorious," Greene wrote to Washington that day.[xxxv] But almost immediately, Morgan recognized the danger to his army. Burdened with British prisoners and captured stores, Morgan began his retreat north by northwest shortly after the battle. A dejected Cornwallis, now united with Leslie's reinforcements, pursued Morgan, though by the time he finally marched his lumbering army, it was already January 19th, and Morgan had gained a considerable head start. Still, the ever cautious Greene sensed danger and immediately prepared his force on the Pee Dee to march toward Morgan.

This would set in motion the "Race to the Dan," Cornwallis's attempt to overcome Greene in flight, followed by their eventual confrontation at Guilford Courthouse in March 1781. The bloody stalemate there would convince Cornwallis his prospects for cutting off the south were better served in eastern Virginia, leading him into Washington's trap at Yorktown.

We can argue that, in the face of American perseverance, the British would have ultimately yielded their claim on the American colonies no matter the outcome at Cowpens. Perhaps you could say it was only a matter of time. But we don't have to conduct such deliberations. From the fields of Cowpens we can draw a direct line to the surrender at Yorktown, a contour that altered history and set the foundation for America. In the pages that follow you will read many different accounts of that astonishing moment, some from people who were there, and some from people who early recognized its significance and captured its details for the sake of history. Some of these accounts are biased; some critical.

Some set the stage for the battle to come; and some describe its outcomes. All of them recognized the turning point Cowpens had made in the American cause.

Chapter Notes

[i] David Ramsay, The History of the Revolution of South Carolina, Vol. 2 (Trenton, NJ: Isaac Collins, 1785), 200; Charles Stedman, *The History of the Origin, Progress, and Termination of the American War, Volume II* (London: Printed for the Author, 1794), 325.

[ii] John Buchanan, *The Road to Guilford Courthouse: The American Revolution in the Carolinas* (New York: John Wiley & Sons, 1997), 329.

[iii] Mark M. Boatner III, *Encyclopedia of the American Revolution* (Mechanicsburg, PA: Stackpole Books edition, 1994), 298.

[iv] "Nathanael Greene (hereafter NG) to George Washington, December 7, 1780," *The Papers of Nathanael Greene* (hereafter *NG*), Edited by Dennis M. Conrad and Richard K. Showman. Chapel Hill, NC: The University of North Carolina Press, 1995), Vol. 6, 543 (hereafter notated as volume:page(s), as in 6:543).

[v] "George Washington to NG, November 8, 1780," *NG*, 6:469; also "Marquis de Lafayette to NG, November 10, 1780," *NG*, 6:476-477.

[vi] Sydney G. Fisher, *The Struggle for American Independence* (Philadelphia: Lippincott, 1908), 2:377. Quoted by Ward, *The War of the Revolution*, 2:751.

[vii] "Greene to Morgan, December 16, 1780," *Cowpens Papers, Being Correspondence of General Morgan and the Prominent Actors* (Charleston, SC: The News & Courier, 1881), 9-11.

[viii] "NG to an Unidentified Person, January 1-23, 1781," *NG*, 7:175.

[ix] "Cornwallis to Rawdon, December 26, 1780," *The Cornwallis Papers: The Campaigns of 1780 and 1781 in the Southern Theater of*

the American Revolutionary War, edited by Ian Saberton (East Sussex, England: The Naval and Military Press Ltd, 2010), Volume 3, 226-227. (Hereafter notated as *CP*, with volume:pages(s), as in 3:226-227).

[x] "Cornwallis to Rawdon, December 30, 178)," *CP*, 3:232-233.

[xi] "Cornwallis to Clinton, December 22, 1780, *CP*, 3:28-29; also Mark M. Boatner, *Encyclopedia of the American Revolution*, 1038.

[xii] Banastre Tarleton, *A History of the Campaigns of 1781 and 1781, in the Southern Provinces of North America* (London: T. Cadell, 1787), 208.

[xiii] "NG to Francis Marion, December 24, 1780," *NG*, 6:607.

[xiv] Christopher Ward, *The War of the Revolution* (New York: Skyhorse Publishing edition, 2011), 167.

[xv] Mark M. Boatner, *Encyclopedia of the American Revolution*, 735-736.

[xvi] Lawrence E. Babits, *A Devil of a Whipping: The Battle of Cowpens* (Chapel Hill, NC: University of North Carolina Press, 1998), 24.

[xvii] M.F. Treacy, *Prelude to Yorktown: The Southern Campaign of Nathanael Greene* (Chapel Hill, NC: University of North Carolina Press, 1963), 79.

[xviii] "Daniel Morgan to Nathanael Greene, January 15, 1780," *NG*, 7:127.

[xix] Christopher Ward, *The War of the Revolution*, 701.

[xx] "Tarleton to Cornwallis, January 4, 1781"; and "Cornwallis to Tarleton, January 5, 1781"; from *A History of the Campaigns of 1781 and 1781*, Banastre Tarleton, 245-246.

[xxi] Thomas Young, "Memoir of Thomas Young, a Revolutionary Patriot of South Carolina," *Orion 3* (October & November 1843).

[xxii] William Johnson, *Sketches of the Life and Correspondence of Nathanael Greene: Major General of the Armies of the United States in the war of the Revolution* (Charleston, SC: A.E. Miller, 1822), 376.

[xxiii] John Buchanan, *The Road to Guilford Courthouse*, 315.

[xxiv] Don Higginbotham, *Daniel Morgan: Revolutionary Rifleman* (Chapel Hill, NC: University of North Carolina Press, 1961),

133-134.

[xxv] John Buchanan, *The Road to Guilford Courthouse*, 316.

[xxvi] M.F. Treacy, *Prelude to Yorktown*, 96.

[xxvii] Thomas Young, "Memoir of Thomas Young."

[xxviii] James Collins, "Autobiography of a Revolutionary Soldier," revised and prepared by John M. Roberts (Clinton, LA: Feliciana Democrat, 1859).

[xxix] John Buchanan, *The Road to Guilford Courthouse*, 324.

[xxx] James Graham, *The Life of General Daniel Morgan* (New York: Derby & Jackson, 1859), 304.

[xxxi] "Daniel Morgan to Nathanael Greene, January 19, 1781," *Cowpens Papers*, 21-22.

[xxxii] Lawrence E. Babits, *A Devil of a Whipping*, 130.

[xxxiii] Christopher Ward, *War of the Revolution*, 762.

[xxxiv] "Daniel Morgan to Nathanael Greene, January 19, 1781," *Cowpens Papers*, 24.

[xxxv] "Nathanael Greene to George Washington, January 24, 1781," *NG*, 7:181.

Part One: Prelude to Battle

CHAPTER ONE:

CORRESPONDENCE BETWEEN NATHANAEL GREENE, DANIEL MORGAN, AND OTHO HOLLAND WILLIAMS*

The correspondence collected here between Nathanael Greene and his Continental officers reveals both the complexity of Greene's assignment to Daniel Morgan and the struggles Morgan experienced undertaking it. By sending Morgan's "Flying Army" west of the Catawba, Greene wanted Morgan to "spirit up the people," collect provisions, prevent plundering, and keep check on the British Army, though not to "come to action unless you have a manifest superiority and a moral certainty of succeeding." This was no small task, although Morgan experienced some initial success when a detachment of cavalry and local militia routed a band of Loyalists at Hammond's Store on December 30, 2780.

---

* Unless otherwise noted, all correspondence in this section is reprinted from *Cowpens Papers: Being Correspondence of General Morgan and the Prominent Actors*, Theodorus Bailey Myers, ed. (Charleston, SC: The News & Courier, 1881).

But the success at Hammond's Store created additional problems for Morgan. As militia flocked to his camp in early January, he struggled to feed his growing force and forage his horses. His efforts to secure provisions ignited a quarrel with Thomas Sumter, South Carolina's brigadier general of militia. To Greene he proposed an expedition west to Georgia, more to keep his men active than for any military objective. Greene reluctantly agreed, though his anxiety was palpable. By this time, unbeknownst to Greene, the end game was in play. Morgan had received word that Banastre Tarleton was in pursuit. His letter to Greene of January 15, 1781, reveals the strategic considerations that inspired his initial retreat, then led him into battle on the fateful morning of January 17. If Morgan's despondency alarms us, we must remember he was suffering from debilitating sciatica, or rheumatism, brought on by weeks of camp life and heavy rain. His men were freezing and starving, some of them in bare feet. But as we shall read in subsequent sections, the "Old Wagoner" still had a few tricks up his sleeve, and he would play them to perfection in the battle to come.

Nathanael Greene to Daniel Morgan, December 16, 1780

Sir—You are appointed to the command of a corps of Light Infantry, a detachment of Militia, and Lt. Col. Washington's Regiment of Light Dragoons. With these troops you will proceed to the West side of the Catawba river, where you will be joined by a body of Volunteer Militia under the command of Brig. Genl. Davidson of this State, and by the Militia lately under the command of Brig. Genl. Sumter. This force, and such others as may join you from Georgia, you will employ against the enemy on the West side of the River, either offensively or defensively as your own prudence and discretion may direct, acting with caution, and avoiding surprizes by every possible precaution. For the present I give you the entire command in that quarter, and do hereby require all Officers and Soldiers engaged in the American cause to be subject to your orders and command. The object of this detachment is to give protection to that part of the country and spirit up the people—to annoy the enemy in that quarter—collect the provisions and forage out of the way of the enemy, which you will have formed into a number of small magazines, in or near the position you may think proper to take. You will prevent plundering as much as possible, and be as careful of your provisions and forage as may be, giving receipts for whatever you take to all such as are friends to the independence of America. Should the enemy move in force towards the Pedee, where this Army will take a position, you will move in such direction as to enable you to join me if necessary, or to fall upon the flank or into the rear of the enemy as occasion may require. You will spare no pains to get good intelligence of the Enemy's situation, and keep me constantly advertized of both your and their movements. You will appoint for the time being a Quarter Master, Commissary and Forage Master, who will follow your instructions in their several lines.

Confiding in your abilities and activity, I entrust you with this command, being persuaded you will do everything in your power to distress the enemy and afford protection to the country.

Given under my hand at Charlotte, this 16th of December, 1780.

NATH. GREENE

Greene to Morgan, December 29, 1780

Camp at the Cheraws
on the East Side of Pedee

Dear Sir—We arrived here on the 26th inst., after a very tedious and disagreeable march, owing to the badness of the roads and the poor and weak state of our teams. Our prospects with regard to provisions are mended, but this is no Egypt.

I have this moment received intelligence that General Leslie has landed at Charlestown, and is on his march to

Camden. His force is about 2,000, perhaps something less. I also am informed Lord Cornwallis has collected his troops at Camden. You will watch their motions very narrowly, and take care and guard against a surprize. Should they move in force this way you will endeavor to cross the river and join us. Do not be sparing of your Expresses, but let me know as often as possible of your situation. I wish to be fully informed of your prospect respecting provisions, and also the number of militia that have joined you.

A large number of tents and hatchets are on the road. As soon as they arrive you shall be supplied. Many other articles necessary for the Army, particularly shoes, are coming on.

I am, sir,
Your humble servant,

NATH. GREENE

Adjutant-General Otho Holland Williams to Daniel Morgan, December 30, 1780

Camp Hicks Creek on P.D.

Dr. General—I enclose you a number of letters by a Sergeant of Lt. Col. Washington's Regt., which I hope will arrive safe. We are at present in a Camp of Repose, and the General is exerting himself and every Body else to put his little Army in a better condition. Tents in sufficient number for a larger army than ours are coming from Philadelphia. They are expected to arrive early in January. We also expect a number of shoes, shirts and some other articles essentially necessary.

Col. Marion writes the General that Gen. Leslie landed with his command at Chas. town on the 20th inst., and that he had advanced as far as Monk's Corner. You know Lord Cornwallis has collected his force in Camden, probably they mean to form a junction and attempt to give a blow to a part of our force, while we are divided, and most probably that blow will be aimed at you, as our position in the centre of a wilderness is less accessible than your camp. I know your discretion renders all caution from me unnecessary, but my Friendship will plead an excuse for the impertinence of wishing you to run no risque of a Defeat. May your Laurels flourish when your Locks fade, and an age of Peace reward your toils in War. My love to every Fellow Soldier, and Adieu.

Yrs. mo. truly,

O. H. WILLIAMS.

Daniel Morgan to Nathanael Greene, January 4, 1781

Camp on Pacolet

Dear Sir—As soon as I could form a just Judgment of our Situation and the Prospects, I dispatched Colonel Malmady to give you the necessary Information, and I flatter myself he has done it to your satisfaction. The Accounts he brings you of Lieut. Col. Washington's success at Hammond's Store is as authentic as any I have been able to collect. It was followed by some small advantages. Gen. Cunningham, on hearing of Waters' defeat[*], prepared to evacuate Fort Williams, and had just marched out with the last of his garrison as a party consisting of about forty Militia Horsemen, under Colonel Hayes, and ten dragoons, under Mr. Simmons, arrived with an Intention of demanding a Surrender. The Enemy's force was so superior to theirs that they could effect nothing more than the demolition of the Fort.

---

[*] Morgan's reports suggested the Loyalists at Hammond's Store were led by a Georgian named Thomas Waters.

Sensible of the Importance of guarding against Surprizes I have used every precaution of this Head. I have had men who were recommended as every way calculated for the business constantly watching the Motions of the Enemy, so that unless they deceive me I am in no danger of being surprized.

I have received no acquisition of force since I wrote to you but expect in a few days to be joined by Col. Clarke and Twiggs Regiment. Their numbers I can not ascertain.

The men on the North side of Broad River I have not yet ordered to join me, but have directed their officers to keep them in Compact Bodies that they may be ready to march at the shortest notice. I intend these as a check on the Enemy should they attempt anything against my Detachment.

My Situation is far from being agreeable to my Wishes or Expectations. Forage and Provisions are not to be had. Here we cannot subsist so that we have but one alternative, either to retreat or move into Georgia. A retreat will be attended with the most fatal consequences. The Spirit which now begins to pervade the People and call them into the Field will be destroyed. The Militia who have already joined will desert us, and it is not improbable that a Regard for their own Safety will induce them to join the Enemy.

I shall await with impatience for your directions on the subject of my letter by Colonel Malmady, as till then my operations must be in a manner suspended.

I am, dear sir, your obedient servant,

D. MORGAN

BATTLE OF COWPENS

Nathanael Greene to Daniel Morgan, January 8, 1781

Camp S. Carolina
Ferry on the East Side of Pedee

DEAR SIR—Col. Malmady arrived here yesterday with your letter of the 31st of December. Nothing could have afforded more pleasure than the successful attack of Lieut. Col. Washington upon the Tories.* I hope it will be attended with a happy influence upon both Whig and Tory, to the reclaiming of one and the encouragement of the other. I wish you to forward to me an official report as soon as possible, that I may send it to the Northward. I have maturely considered your proposition of an expedition into Georgia, and cannot think it warrantable in the critical situation our Army is in. I have no small reason to think, by intelligence from different quarters, that the enemy have a movement in contemplation, and in all probability it will be this way, from the impudence of the Tories, who are collecting in different quarters in the most inaccessible swamps and morasses. Should you go into Georgia and the enemy push this way, your whole force will be useless. The enemy having no objects there but what is secure in their fortifications will take no notice of your movement, but serve you as General Provost did General Lincoln, oblige you to return by making a forward movement themselves, and you will be so far in the rear that you can do them no injury. But if you continue in the neighborhood of the place you now are, and they attempt to push forward, you may intercept their communications with Charlestown, or harass their rear, both of which will alarm the enemy not a little.

If you employ detachments to intercept supplies going to Ninety-Six and Augusta it will perplex the enemy very much. If you think Ninety-Six, Augusta or even Savannah can be surprized, and your force will admit of a detachment for the

---

* Another reference to the action at Hammond's Store.

purpose and leave you sufficiency to keep up a good countenance, you may attempt it. But don't think of attempting either unless by surprize, for you will only beat your heads against the wall without success. Small parties are better to effect the purpose than large bodies, and the success will not greatly depend upon the numbers, but on the secrecy and spirit of the attack.

I must repeat my caution to you to guard against a surprize. You say the enemy and the Tories both will try to bring you into disgrace, if possible to prevent your influence upon the militia, especially the weak and wavering.

I cannot pretend to give you any particular instructions respecting a position. But somewhere between the Saluda and the north branch of Broad River appears the most favorable for annoying the enemy, interrupting their supplies and harrassing their rear if they should make a movement this way. If you could detach a small party to kill the enemy's draught horses and recruiting cavalry upon the Congaree, it would give them almost as deadly a blow as a defeat. But this matter must be conducted with great secrecy and dispatch. Lieut-Col. Lee[*] has just arrived with his legion, and Col. Greene is within a few days march of this with a reinforcement. The order is given to Capt. Marbury to make the pack saddles at Salisbury. I wish you to have Lieut. Col. Washington's horse kept in as good order as possible, and let the militia light horse do all the fatigue duty. We may want a body of heavy cavalry, and if they are broken down on common duty we shall have nothing to depend upon. I have ordered Major Campbell, who is at Salisbury with 100 Virginia riflemen, to join you.

I am, dear sir, your most obedient humble servant.

NATH. GREENE.

---

[*] For more on the service of Lieutenant-colonel Henry "Light Horse Harry" Lee in the Southern Campaign, see Chapter 12.

Daniel Morgan to Nathanael Greene, January 15, 1781*

Camp at Burr's Mills, Thicketty Creek

Dear General—Your letters of the 3rd and 8th instant came to hand yesterday, just as I was preparing to change my position; was therefore obliged to detain the express until this evening.

The accounts I have transmitted you of Lieut. Col. Washington's success, accords with his opinion. The number killed and wounded on the part of the tories must depend on conjecture, as they broke on the first charge, scattered through the woods, and were pursued in every direction. The consequences attending to the defeat will be fatal to the disaffected. They have not been able to embody.

Sensible of the importance of having magazines of forage and provisions established in this country, I have left no means in my power unessayed to effect this business. I dispatched Captain Chitty (whom I have appointed as commissary of purchases for my command), with orders to collect and store all the provisions that could be obtained between the Catawba and Broad rivers. I gave him directions to call on Col. Hill, who commands a regiment of militia in that quarter, to furnish him with a proper number of men to assist him in the execution of this commission; but he, to my great surprise, has just returned without effecting anything. He tells me that his failure proceeded from the want of the countenance and assistance of Col. Hill, who assured him that General Sumter directed him to obey no orders from me, unless they came through him.†

---

* From *The Life of General Daniel Morgan: Of the Virginia Line of the Army of the United States, with Portions of his Correspondence* by James Graham (New York: Derby & Jackson, 1859).

† Col. William Hill was a South Carolina militia leader and associate of militia general Thomas Sumter. This passage refers to a dispute between Sumter and Greene about the order of the command in the Southern Campaign, with Sumter asserting his rank was superior to Morgan's.

I find it impracticable to procure more provisions in this quarter than are absolutely necessary for our own immediate consumption; Indeed it has been with the greatest difficulty that we have been able to effect this. We have to feed such a number of horses, that the most plentiful country must soon be exhausted. Nor am I a little apprehensive that no part of this State accessible to us can support us long. Could the militia be persuaded to change their fatal mode of going to war, much provision might be saved; but the custom has taken such deep root that it cannot be abolished.*

Upon a full and mature deliberation, I am confirmed in the opinion that nothing can be effected by my detachment in this country, which will balance the risks I will be subjected to by remaining here. The enemy's great superiority in numbers, and our distance from the main army, will enable Lord Cornwallis to detach so superior a force against me, as to render it essential to our safety to avoid coming to action. Nor will this be always in my power. No attempt to surprise me will be left untried by them; and situated as we must be, ever possible precaution may not be sufficient to secure us. The scarcity of forage renders it impossible for us always to be in a compact body; and were this not the case, it is beyond the art of man to keep the militia from straggling. These reasons induce me to request that I may be recalled with my detachment, and that Gen. Davidson and Col. Pickens may be left with the militia of North and South Carolina and Georgia. They will not be so much the object of the enemy's attention, and will be capable of being a check on the disaffected, which is all I can effect.

Col. Pickens is a valuable, discreet and attentive officer, and has the confidence of the militia.

My force is inadequate to the attempts you have hinted at. I have now with me only two hundred South Carolina and

---

* Morgan is referring to the militia's practice of traveling by horse, whose forage put strains on the Continental supply chain and denuded the local countryside.

Georgia, and one hundred and forty North Carolina, volunteers. Nor do I expect to have more than two-thirds of these to assist me, should I be attacked, for it is impossible to keep them collected.

Though I am convinced that were you on the spot, the propriety of my proposition would strike you forcibly; should you think it unadvisable to recall me, you may depend on my attempting everything to annoy the enemy, and to provide for the safety of the detachment I shall cheerfully acquiesce in your determination.

Col. Tarleton has crossed the Tyger at Musgrove's Mill; his force we cannot learn. It is more than probable we are his object. Cornwallis, by last accounts, was at the cross-roads near Lee's old place.

We have just learned that Tarleton's force is from eleven to twelve hundred British.

I am, dear general,
Truly yours,

DANIEL MORGAN

*Nathanael Greene to Daniel Morgan, January 19, 1781**

Camp on Pedee

Dear Sir—Your favor of the 15th was delivered to me last evening about 12 o'clock. I am surprized that General Sumter should give such an order as you mention to Col. Hill, nor can I persuade myself but that there must be some mistake in the matter, for tho' it is the most military to convey orders through the principal to the dependents, as well from propriety as respect, yet this may not always be convenient or even

---

* Though the Battle of Cowpens occurred on January 17, 1781, Greene would not receive word of the victory until January 23.

practicable, and, therefore, to give a positive order not to obey was repugnant to reason and common sence. As the head was subject to your orders, consequently the dependents also. I will write General Sumter on the subject, but as it is better to conciliate than agrevate matters where everything depends so much on voluntary principles, I wish you to take no notice of the matter, but endeavor to influence his conduct to give you all the aid in his power. Write him frequently and consult with him freely. He is a man of great pride and considerable merit, and should not be neglected. If he has given such order, I persuade myself he will see the impropriety of the matter and correct it in future, unless personal glory is more the object than public good, which I cannot suppose is the case with him or any other man who fights in the cause of Liberty. I was informed of Lord Cornwallis' movements before the arrival of your letter, and agree with you in opinion that you are the object; and from the making so general a movement it convinces me he feels a great inconvenience from your force and situation. Gen. Leslie has crossed the Catawba to join him. He would never harrass his troops to remove you if he did not think it an object of some importance. Nor would he put his collective force in motion if he had not some respect for your numbers. I am sensible your situation is critical, and requires the most watchful attention to guard against a surprize. But I think it is of great importance to keep up a force in that quarter, nor can I persuade myself that the militia alone will answer the same valuable purposes as when joined by the Continental Troops.

It is not my wish you should come to action unless you have a manifest superiority and a moral certainty of succeeding. Put nothing to the hazard, a retreat may be disagreeable but not disgraceful. Regard not the opinion of the day. It is not our business to risque too much, our affairs are in too critical a situation and require time and nursing to give them a better tone.

If General Sumter and you could fix upon a plan for him to hold the post which you now occupy, to be joined by the militia under General Davidson, and you with your force, the Georgia and Virginia militia to move toward Augusta or into that quarter, I should have no objection to such a movement; provided you think it will answer any valuable purpose, and can be attempted with a degree of safety. I am unwilling to recall you if it can be avoided, but I had rather recall you by far than to expose you to the hazard of a surprize.

Before they can possibly reach you I imagine the movements of Lord Cornwallis and Col. Tarleton will be sufficiently explained, and you obliged to take some decisive measure. I shall be perfectly satisfied if you keep clear of a misfortune, for, tho' I wish you laurels, yet I am unwilling to expose the common cause to give you an opportunity to acquire them.

As the rivers are subject to sudden and great swells, you must be careful that the enemy do not take a position to gain your rear when you can neither retreat by your flank or front. The Pedee rose 25 feet for the last week in 30 hours. I am preparing boats to move always with the army. Would one or two be of use to you? They will be put upon four wheels, and may be moved with little more difficulty than a loaded waggon.

Gen. Davidson is desired to receive orders, and in conjunction with Gen. Sumter to consult with you, a plan for a combined attack on one of the divisions of Lord Cornwallis's army, and also respecting your movements into Georgia.

I am, with esteem, dear sir,
Your most obedient, humble servant,

NATH. GREENE

CHAPTER TWO:

CORRESPONDENCE BETWEEN BANASTRE TARLETON AND CHARLES, LORD CORNWALLIS*

Though initially unconcerned about Morgan's move to the west, Cornwallis began to fear for the safety of the British garrison at Ninety Six following the skirmish at Hammond's Store on December 30, 1780. The correspondence here outlines Cornwallis and Tarleton's plans to drive Morgan from their western flank: As Tarleton's pursuit pushed Morgan to the east side of the Broad River, Cornwallis would also move northward to catch Morgan in a vise.

But this correspondence ultimately reveals also the issues plaguing the British Army that would contribute to their doom in the Southern Campaign: the complicated logistics required to move an army's baggage

---

* From *A History of the Campaigns of 1780 and 1781, in the Southern Provinces of North America* by Banastre Tarleton (London: Printed for T. Cadell, 1787).

and men; bad weather and non-existent roads; unreliable communications; the random happenstances of campaigning in unknown country. After the war, Tarleton would claim Cornwallis was aware that he had initiated his pursuit of Morgan, leading to the confrontation at Cowpens on January 17. As we shall later read, Cornwallis was reluctant to criticize his young protégé, but the evidence supporting Tarleton's claims is thin. Whatever the communication, or miscommunication, Cornwallis did not move to spring the trap, and ultimately Morgan was able to not only destroy Tarleton, but also rejoin with Greene after the battle.

Earl Cornwallis to Lieutenant-Colonel Tarleton, December 30th, 1780

Dear Tarleton—I send you the reports of the day. First, Morgan and Washington have passed Broad river; secondly, a brig from York says, that a packet had arrived there from England, and that accounts were brought, that six regiments were under orders for embarkation, supposed to be defined for Carolina; thirdly, and the worst report of all, if true, that one thousand French are got into Cape Fear, who will probably fortify themselves at Wilmington, and stop our water communication with Charles town for provisions; fourthly, that an embarkation was taking place, under General Phillips, from New York, said to be destined for the Chesapeak.

Lord Rawdon mentions, that by a letter from McKinnon to England, he is afraid that the accoutrements for the 17th dragoons are coming up by the slow process of General Leslie's corps. Try to get all possible intelligence of Morgan.

Your's very sincerely,

CORNWALLIS

BATTLE OF COWPENS

Earl Cornwallis to Lieutenant-Colonel Tarleton, January 2, 1780

Dear Tarleton—I sent Haldane to you last night, to desire you would pass Broad river, with the legion and the first battalion of the 71st, as soon as possible. If Morgan is still at Williams'*, or any where within your reach, I should wish you to push him to the utmost: I have not heard from McArthur, of his having cannon; nor would I believe it, unless he has it from good authority: It is, however, possible, and Ninety Six is of so much consequence, that no time is to be lost.

Your's sincerely,

CORNWALLIS.

Let me know if you think that the moving the whole, or any part of my corps, can be of use.

---

* "Williams'" was a Loyalist stockade on the captured property of James Williams, a Patriot militia commander killed at King's Mountain. After routing the Loyalists at Hammond's Store on December 30, 1780, elements of Morgan's Continental command supported by Patriot militia attacked the Loyalist fort at Williams's farm on December 31. The Loyalist evacuated the fort and retreated to Ninety Six, causing concern among the British command that Ninety Six would be attacked next.

BATTLE OF COWPENS

Lieutenant-Colonel Tarleton to Earl Cornwallis (extract), January 4, 1781

Morgan, with upwards of one thousand two hundred men, being on this side Broad river, to threaten Ninety Six, and evade your lordship's army whenever you may move, I beg leave to offer my opinion how his design may be prevented.

I must draw my baggage, the 71st and legion's are deposited at my old camp,* to me. I wish it to be escorted by the 17th light dragoons, for whom horses are ready; by the yagers, if to be spared; and by the 7th regiment. The 7th I will send, as soon as I reach Ennoree, with the field piece, to Ninety Six. My encampment is now twenty miles from Brierley's, in a plentiful forage country, and I can lay in four days flour for a move.

When I advance, I must either destroy Morgan's corps, or push it before me over Broad river, towards King's mountain. The advance of the army should commence (when your lordship orders this corps to move) onwards for King's mountain. Frequent communication by letter can pass the Broad river. I feel myself bold in offering my opinion, as it flows from zeal for the public service, and well-grounded inquiry concerning the enemy's designs and operations.

I have directed Captain McPherson, the bearer of this letter, who is going on the recruiting service, to deliver a letter to Lieutenant Munroe, whom I left at my camp, to bring up my baggage, but no women.

---

* The British 71st Regiment was an infantry regiment raised in Scotland in 1775 and disbanded in 1786. The "legion" referred to here is the British Legion; for more information about the British Legion, see the "Introduction."

If your lordship approves of this plan, Captain McPherson may give my order to Lieutenant Munroe to escort to me three puncheons of rum, and some salt; and, upon their arrival, I will move.

Earl Cornwallis to Lieutenant-Colonel Tarleton, January 5, 1781

Dear Tarleton—Since I wrote to you this morning, I received yours dated yesterday, two P. M. You have exactly done what I wished you to do; and understood my intentions perfectly. Lest my letter of this morning should miscarry, I repeat the most material paragraph.

Your baggage is ordered to Brierley's, under care of Seventh regiment. I propose marching on Sunday.

Yours sincerely,

CORNWALLIS

Earl Cornwallis to Lieutenant-Colonel Tarleton, January 11, 1781

I received yours last night of the 9th*, four P.M. I fear the waters have been much more swelled since you wrote it. At present I think I will move Saturday† to cross roads. I can hear

---

* Tarleton's letter of January 9 has not been preserved.

† Cornwallis writes here on Thursday, January 11, indicating he plans to move on Saturday, January 13. Cornwallis did in fact break camp from his winter headquarters at Winnsboro on January 8, but by January 17, he had only traveled forty miles to Turkey Creek, where they camped at the farm of William Hillhouse, about twenty miles east of modern-day Rock Hill, South Carolina.

nothing of Morgan; they say there are several ferries high up on Broad river where he may pass, particularly Talbot's ferry. Leslie is much retarded by waters.

Yours sincerely,

CORNWALLIS

Part Two: Primary Accounts

CHAPTER THREE:

From
*A JOURNAL OF THE SOUTHERN EXPEDITION**
by WILLIAM SEYMOUR

William Seymour was a sergeant major in the famed Delaware Regiment. Most of its men had enlisted in 1776 and fought in the important actions of the next three years. In 1780, the regiment was attached to the Maryland Division because of its small size and marched south with General Horatio Gates, where it was decimated at the Battle of Camden on August 16, losing its two senior officers and eight other officers. The Regiment was re-formed into two, 96-man companies; Seymour was assigned to the company commanded by Captain Robert Kirkwood, which was detached westward under Morgan in December 1780. "The Delaware troops . . . had suffered very severely at the defeat of Gates," noted the early Nathanael Greene biographer William Johnson. "This little corps . . . was the admiration of the army, and their leader Kirkwood

---

* William Seymour, "A Journal of the Southern Expedition, 170-1783," *Papers of the Historical Society of Delaware* XV (Wilmington, DE, 1896).

was the American Diomed. Like the Marylanders, they had been enlisted for the war, and like the veterans of that brigade, were not excelled by any troops in America, perhaps the world."

Seymour's Journal is often cited by Cowpens' historians for its account of the march west from the Continental camp in Charlotte, North Carolina, to the Pacolet River in western South Carolina in December 1780. It also provides a graphic description of the wretched condition of Morgan's troops. Not surprisingly, Seymour writes glowingly of Kirkwood, who was never promoted beyond the rank of captain due to the small size of the Delaware Regiment, despite his heroics at Cowpens, Guilford Courthouse, Hobkirk's Hill, and Eutaw Springs.

We lay on this ground[†] from the 22d November till the 17th December, and marched to Charlotte, fifteen miles. Same day General Smallwood set out on his march for Maryland. At this time the troops were in a most shocking condition for the want of clothing, especially shoes, and we having kept open campaign all winter the troops were taking sick very fast. Here the manly fortitude of the troops of the Maryland Line was very great, being obliged to march and do duty barefoot, being all the winter the chief part of them wanting coats and shoes, which they bore with the greatest patience imaginable, for which their praise should never be forgotten; and indeed in all the hardships which they had undergone the never seemed to frown.

General Greene with his troops marched from Charlotte on the 20th December, directing his route towards Chiraw

---

* William Johnson, *Sketches of the Life and Correspondence of Nathanael Greene, Major General of the United States in the War of the Revolution* (Charleston, SC: A.E. Miller, 1822), 445.
† This reference is to the Continental Army camp called Camp New Providence, established by North Carolina militia colonel William Davidson on October 20, 1780. It was located fourteen miles south of Charlotte on Six Mile Creek, near what is today the Mecklenburg and Union county line. General Daniel Morgan's light troops, including Maryland, Delaware, and Virginia Continentals used the camp as a base of operations from October to mid-December 1780.

Hills, in order to procure forage and there spend the remainder of the winter.

On the 21st ult. the troops under General Morgan marched from Charlotte, being joined by two companies of light infantry detached from the Maryland Line, directing our march towards Pacolet River. First day's march from Charlotte we came to Catabo River. Next day we crossed the river at Bitzer's ferry. Next day we marched to Cane Creek; next, being the 24th, we were alarmed at two o'clock in the morning by some men on horseback coming to our advance picquet, at which sentinels challenging and no answer being made, upon which the sentinels fired and afterwards the whole guard, when immediately the whole turned out and continued under arms till daybreak. This day we crossed the Broad River, and the next day, being the 25th, we encamped at Pacolet River.

On the 27th the General received intelligence that Colonel Tarleton was advancing in order to surprise us;* upon which there were strong picquets erected all around the encampment, putting ourselves in the best posture of defence. The rolls were ordered to be called every two hours, and reports given in by those that were absent. We arrived here in five days since we set out on our march from Charlotte, fifty-eight miles, it being very difficult marching in crossing deep swamps and very steep hills, which rendered our march very unpleasant. The inhabitants along this way live very poor, their plantations uncultivated, and living in mean dwellings. They seem chiefly to be offspring of the ancient Irish, being very affable and courteous to strangers.

On the 31st December Colonel Washington was detached to Fort William in order to surprise some Tories that lay there; and meeting with a party of them near said place, upon which ensued a smart engagement, the latter having one hundred and sixty men killed, and thirty-three made prisoners.

---

* Seymour's recollection is faulty here. Cornwallis did not detach Tarleton against Morgan until after the skirmish at Hammond's Store on December 30, 1780.

BATTLE OF COWPENS

On the first day of January, 1781, there was one of the Tories tried and found guilty of desertion to the enemy and piloting the Indians on our army, they making great havoc among them; upon which he was hanged on a tree the same day till he was dead.

On the 4th there was one of Col. Washington's Horse tried and found guilty of desertion to the enemy, when agreeable to his sentence he was shot the same day.

We lay on this ground from the twenty-fifth December, 1780, till the fourteenth of January, 1781, and then proceeded on our march further up the river toward the iron works in order to frustrate the designs of the enemy who were coming round us, Colonel Tarleton on one side and Lord Cornwallis on the other. We encamped on the Cowpen Plains on the evening of the sixteenth January, forty-two miles, being joined by some Georgia volunteers and South [Carolina] Militia, to the number of between two and three hundred. Next day being the seventeenth January, we received intelligence a while before day, that Colonel Tarleton was advancing in our rear in order to give us battle, upon which we were drawn up in order of battle, the men seeming to be in good spirits and very willing to fight. The militia dismounted and were drawn up in front of the standing troops on the right and left flanks, being advanced about two hundred yards. By this time the enemy advanced and attacked the militia in front, which they stood very well for some time till being overpowered by the superior number of the enemy they retreated, but in very good order, not seeming to be in the least confused. By this time the enemy advanced and attacked our light infantry with both cannon and small arms, where meeting with a very warm reception they thought to surround our right flank, to prevent which Captain Kirkwood with his company wheeled to the right and attacked their left flank so vigorously that they were soon repulsed,[*] our

---

[*] Kirkwood and his Delaware soldiers fought bravely at Cowpens, enduring a twenty-five percent casualty rate, higher than any other American unit.

men advancing on them so very rapidly that they soon gave way. Our left flank advanced at the same time and repulsed their right flank, upon which they retreated off, leaving us entire masters of the field, our men pursuing them for the distance of twelve miles, insomuch that all their infantry was killed, wounded, and taken prisoners. This action commenced about seven o'clock in the morning and continued till late in the afternoon.

In the action were killed of the enemy one hundred and ninety men, wounded one hundred eighty, and taken prisoners one Major, thirteen Captains, fourteen Lieutenants, and nine Ensigns, and five hundred and fifty private men, with two field pieces and four standards of colours.* Their heavy baggage would have shared the same fate, if Tarleton, who retreated with his cavalry, had not set fire to it, burning up twenty-six waggons. This victory on our side can be attributed to nothing else but Divine Providence, they having thirteen hundred in the field of their best troops, and we not eight hundred standing troops and militia.

The troops engaged against us were the 7th or Royal English Fuzileers, the First Battalion of the 71st, and the British Legion, horse and foot.

The courage and conduct of the brave General Morgan in this action is highly commendable, as likewise Colonel Howard, who all the time of the action rode from right to left of the line encouraging the men; and indeed all the officers and men behaved with uncommon and undaunted bravery, but more especially the brave Captain Kirkwood and his company, who that day did wonders, rushing on the enemy without either dread or fear, and being instrumental in taking a great number of prisoners.

Our loss in the action were one Lieutenant wounded, and one Sergeant, and thirty-five killed and wounded, of which

---

* See the editor's "Introduction" for what is now regarded as the commonly accepted casualty figures for the Battle.

fourteen were of Captain Kirkwood's Company of the Delaware Regiment.

On the 18th we marched off with the prisoners, directing our course for Salisbury; having crossed the Catabo River on the 23d at Shreve's Ford, and there waited for the prisoners who went another road. On our way hither we had very difficult marching, being very mountainous, the inhabitants, who were chiefly Virginians, living very poor, except one settlement on the other side of the Catabo, being excellent good land and inhabited by Dutch. We remained on this ground till the first February, waiting the motion of the enemy, who this day crossed the river lower down than where we lay, and coming unawares on the militia commanded by Genl. Davidson, on which ensued a smart skirmish in which General Davidson was killed, and a great many more killed and wounded, upon which the militia retreated off in great disorder.*

---

* This is a reference to the Battle of Cowan's Ford, which took place on February 1, 1781, when the British Army under the leadership of Cornwallis forded the Catawba River opposed by Patriot militia.

CHAPTER FOUR:

JAMES SIMON TO WILLIAM WASHINGTON*

James Simon was a Continental lieutenant serving in the cavalry under Colonel William Washington at Cowpens. The following correspondence was related to the pension application of Sergeant Lawrence Everheart, who was captured and wounded during the battle. Everheart was the advanced scout, or vidette, *who was captured by Tarleton's troops prior to the battle. He is mentioned in several of the accounts included in this collection, including Tarleton's, as giving the British information about the American position. The letter provides a detailed account of Washington's cavalry during the battle, including the harrowing capture and escape of Everheart.*

---

* From *Papers Relating Chiefly to the Maryland Line During the Revolution*, Thomas Balch, ed. (Philadelphia: T.K. and PG. Collins, 1857), 45-46.

BATTLE OF COWPENS

at Charleston, November 3, 1803

Dear General:

In reply to your letter of the 23d ultimo, and to the letter which you inclosed for my perusal, I do hereby (not only from recollection, but from a journal now in my possession, which I kept at the time) certify, that about the dawn of the day, on the 17th of January 1781, you selected Sergeant Everheart from your regiment, and thirteen men, who you sent to reconnoitre Lieut.-Col. Tarleton's army. The advanced guard of this army were mounted, as we understood and believed, on some of the fleetest race horses, which he had impressed from their owners, in this country, and which enabled them to take Sergeant Everheart and one of the men; but the other twelve men returned and gave you information of the approach of the enemy. Immediately after the battle of the Cowpens commenced, you well recollect that your first charge was made on the enemy's cavalry (who were cutting down our militia), and whom, after a smart action, you instantly defeated, leaving in the course of ten minutes eighteen of their brave 17th dragoons dead on the spot, and whom, you will recollect, were deserted by Col. Tarleton's legionary cavalry. The former wore an uniform of red and buff, with sheepskin on their caps; the latter wore an uniform of green with black facings. In pursuit of their cavalry, you overtook their artillery, whom you immediately made prisoners; but the drivers of the horses who were galloping off with two three-pounders, you could not make surrender until after repeated commands you, you were obliged to order to be shot. After securing these field pieces, your third charge was made upon the right wing of their army, composed of the legionary infantry, intermixed with the brave 71st, under the command of Major McArthur; and who, under the operation of an universal panic, having been successfully charged on the left of their army by our friend Colonel Howard, instantly surrendered. Immediately after securing the prisoners, your fourth charge was in pursuit of their cavalry, who, finding they could no longer keep Everheart a prisoner, shot him with a pistol on the head, over one of his eyes (I cannot remember which). Being then intermixed with the enemy, Everheart pointed out to me the man who shot him, and on whom a just retaliation was exercised, and who, by my orders, was instantly shot, and his horse, as well as I recollect, given to Everheart, whom I ordered in the rear to the surgeons. It was at this period of action that we sustained the greatest loss of men, Lieutenant Bell having previously taken of with him, in pursuit of the enemy on our left, nearly a fourth part of your regiment. The enemy were obliged to retreat, and were pursued by you twenty-two miles, taking several prisoners and wounded. To the best of my recollection, Sergeant Everheart was so disabled from his wounds that he received a discharge from you, and retired from the army.

CHAPTER FIVE:

From
*THE MEMOIR OF MAJOR THOMAS YOUNG**

Thomas Young was born in Laurens County, South Carolina, in January 1764, but moved with his family to "Union District" (present-day Union County, South Carolina) as a child. At age sixteen, in the Spring of 1780, he joined the Fair Forest militia, commanded by Thomas Brandon, to avenge the death of his brother, John Young, who was killed in a raid by the notorious Tory commander William "Bloody Bill" Cunningham. The Fair Forest regiment covered parts of what is today southern Spartanburg and Union counties in South Carolina and is sometimes referred to as the Second Spartan Regiment due to its close relation to the First Spartan Regiment of Spartanburg County.

His memoir is frequently cited in histories of the Southern Campaign, particularly the following account of Cowpens. Included also is his account of the engagement at Hammond's Store on December 30.

---

* Thomas Young, "The Memoir of Major Thomas Young," *Orion Magazine*, 1843.

Daniel Morgan reported to Nathanael Greene that 150 Tories were killed at Hammond's Store, without a single Patriot loss; Young's account famously provides context for the butchery that must have facilitated such slaughter.*

Vivid, visceral, and anecdotal, Young's Cowpens reminiscence includes hand-to-hand combat, a perilous escape, and anecdotal encounters with both Daniel Morgan and Banastre Tarleton. Also of note is his depiction of Daniel Morgan's fireside bonhomie the night before the battle, as well as his courageous leadership during it. With only a few exceptions to enhance clarity, Young's original spelling and punctuation are retained. Some paragraph breaks have been added.

The next engagement I was at Hammond's store, on Bush River, somewhere near '96.† Gen. Morgan was encamped at Grindall Shoals to keep the tories in check. He dispatched Col. Washington with a detachment of militia, and about seventy dragoons [mounted infantrymen], to attack a body of tories, who had been plundering the whigs. We came up with them at Hammond's store; in fact, we picked up several scattering ones, within about three miles of the place, from whom we learned all about their position.

When we came in sight, we perceived that the tories had formed in line on the brow of the hill opposite to us. We had a long hill to descend and another to rise. Col. Washington and his dragoons gave a shout, drew swords, and charged down the hill like madmen. The tories fled in every direction without firing a gun. We took a great many prisoners and killed a few. Here I must relate an incident which occurred on this occasion. In Washington's corps there was a boy of fourteen or fifteen, a mere lad, who in crossing Tiger River was ducked by a blunder of his horse. The men laughed and jeered at him very much, at which he got very mad, and swore that boy or no

---

* "Daniel Morgan to Nathanael Greene," December 31, 1780, *The Papers of Nathanael Greene*, Volume VII, 30-31.

† This is a reference to the British garrison at Ninety Six.

boy, he would kill a man that day or die. He accomplished the former. I remember very well being highly amused at the little fellow charging round a crib after a tory, cutting and slashing away with his puny arm, till he brought him down.

We then returned to Morgan's encampment at Grindall Shoals, on the Packolette, and there we remained, eating beef and scouting through the neighborhood until we heard of Tarlton's approach. Having received intelligence that Col. Tarlton designed to cross the Packolette at Easternood Shoals above us, Gen. Morgan broke up his encampment early in the morning of the 16th, and retreated up the mountain road by Hancock's Ville, taking the left hand road not far above, in a direction toward the head of Thickety Creek. We arrived at the field of the Cowpens about sun-down, and were told that there we should meet the enemy. The news was received with great joy by the army. We were very anxious for battle, and many a hearty curse had been vented against Gen. Morgan during that day's March, for retreating, as we thought, to avoid a fight. Night came upon us, yet much remained to be done. It was all important to strengthen the cavalry. Gen. Morgan knew well the power of Tarlton's legion, and he was too wily an officer not to prepare himself as well as circumstances would admit. Two companies of volunteers were called for. One was raised by Major Jolly of Union District, and the other, I think, by Major McCall. I attached myself to Major Jolly's company. We drew swords that night, and were informed we had authority to press any horse not belonging to a dragoon or an officer, into our service for the day.

It was upon this occasion I was more perfectly convinced of Gen.'s qualifications to command militia, than I had ever before been. He went among the volunteers, helped them fix their swords, joked with them about their sweet-hearts, told them to keep in good spirits, and the day would be ours. And long after I laid down, he was going about among the soldiers encouraging them, and telling them that the old wagoner would crack his whip over Ben. (Tarleton) in the morning, as sure as they lived.

BATTLE OF COWPENS

"Just hold your heads, boys, three fires," he would say, "and you are free, and then when you return to your homes, how the old folks will bless you, and the girls kiss you, for your gallant conduct!" I don't believe he slept a wink that night!

But to the battle. Our pickets were stationed three miles in advance. Samuel Clowney was one of the picket guard, and I often heard him afterwards laugh at his narrow escape. Three of Washington's dragoons were out on a scout, when they came almost in contact with the advanced guard of the British army; they wheeled, and were pursued almost into camp. Two got in safely; one poor fellow, whose horse fell down, was taken prisoner. It was about day that the pickets were driven in.

The morning of the 17th of January, 1781, was bitterly cold. We were formed in order of battle, and the men were slapping their hands together to keep warm—an exertion not long necessary.

The battle field was almost a plain with a ravine on both hands, and very little under growth in front or near us. The regulars, under the command of Colonel Howard, a brave man, were formed in two ranks, their right flank resting upon the head of the ravine on the right. The militia were formed on the left of the regulars, under command of Colonel Pickens, their left flank resting near the head of the ravine on the left. The cavalry formed in rear of the center, or rather in rear of the left wing of the regulars.[*] About sunrise, the British line advanced at a sort of trot, with a loud halloo. It was the most beautiful line I ever saw. When they shouted, I heard Morgan say, "They give us the British halloo, boys, give them the Indian halloo, by G--," and he galloped along the lines, cheering the men, and telling them not to fire until we could see the whites of their eyes. Every officer was crying, "Don't

---

[*] Young's description idiosyncratically orients the Patriot lines in relation to ravines running along the west and east sides of the battlefield, rather than the south-to-north orientation in most accounts.

fire," for it was a hard matter for us to keep from it. I should have said the British line advanced under cover of their artillery; for it opened so fiercely upon the center, that Colonel Washington moved his cavalry from the center towards the right wing. The militia fired first. It was, for a time, *pop-pop-pop*, and then a whole volley; but when the regulars fired, it seemed like one sheet of flame from right to left. Oh, it was beautiful!

I have heard old Colonel Fair say often that he believed John Savage fired the first gun in this battle. He was riding to and from, along the lines, when he saw Savage fix his eye upon a British officer; he stepped out of the ranks, raised his gun, fired, and he saw the officer fall. After the first fire, the militia retreated, and the cavalry covered their retreat. They were again formed and renewed the attack, and we retired to the rear. They fought some time. In this I can hardly be mistaken, for I recollect well that the cavalry was twice, during the action, between our army and the enemy. I have understood that one of the retreats was ordered by mistake by one of Morgan's officers. How true this is I cannot say. After the hottest of it, I saw Colonel [Thomas] Brandon coming at full speed to the rear and waving his sword to Colonel Washington. In a moment the command to charge was given, and I soon found that the British cavalry had charged the American right. We made a most furious charge, and cutting through the British cavalry, wheeled and charged them in the rear. In this charge, I exchanged my tackey [pony] for the finest horse I ever rode; it was the quickest swap I ever made in my life!* At this moment the bugle sounded. We, about half-formed and making a sort of circuit at full speed, came up in rear of the British line, shouting and charging like madmen. At this moment Colonel Howard gave the word "charge bayonets!" and the day was

---

* Young's account highlights an unusual aspect of Cowpens: the use of Patriot militia as mounted troops. Though the southern militia's devotion to their horses was notorious, stretching thin Continental forage supplies, they typically fought as infantry, as at King's Mountain.

ours. The British broke, and throwing down their guns and cartouche boxes, made for the wagon road, and did the prettiest sort of running!

After this Major Jolly and seven or eight of us resolved upon an excursion to capture some of the baggage. We went about 12 miles, and captured two British soldiers, two Negroes, and two horses laden with portmanteaus. One of the portmanteaus belonged to a paymaster in the British service and contained gold. Jolly insisted upon my returning with the prize to camp, while he pursued a little farther. I did so. Jolly's party dashed onward, and soon captured an armorer's wagon, with which they became so much engaged that they forgot all about me. I rode along for some miles at my leisure, on my fine gray charger, talking to my prisoners, when, all at once, I saw, coming in advance, a party, which I soon discovered to be British. I knew it was no time to consider now; so I wheeled, put spurs to my horse, and made down the road in hopes of meeting Jolly and his party. My horse was stiff, however, from the severe exercise I had given him that morning, and I soon found that they were gaining upon me. I wheeled abruptly to the right into a cross road, but a party of three or four dashed through the woods and intercepted me. It was now a plain case, and I drew my sword and made battle. I never fought so hard in my life. I knew it was death anyhow, and I resolved to sell my life as dearly as possible.

In a few minutes one finger on my left hand was split open; then I received a cut on my sword arm by a parry which disabled it. In the next instance a cut from a sabre across my forehead, (the scar of which I shall carry to my grave), the skin slipped down over my eyes, and the blood blinded me so that I could see nothing. Then came a thrust in the right shoulder blade, then a cut upon the left shoulder, and a last cut (which you can feel for yourself) on the back of my head—and I fell upon my horse's neck. They took me down, bound up my wounds, and placed me again on my horse a prisoner of war.

When they joined the party in the main road, there were two tories who knew me very well—Littlefield and Kelly.

Littlefield cocked his gun, and swore he would kill me. In a moment nearly twenty British soldiers drew their swords, and cursing him for a d----d coward, for wanting to kill a boy without arms and a prisoner, ran him off. Littlefield did not like me, and for a very good reason. While we were at Grindall Shoals with Morgan, he once caught me out, and tried to take my gun away from me. I knocked him down with it, and as he rose I clicked it, and told him if he didn't run I'd blow him through. He did not long hesitate which of the two to choose.

I asked Kelly not to tell the British who I was, and I do not think the fellow did. Col. Tarlton sent for me, and I rode by his side for several miles. He was a very fine looking man, with rather a proud bearing, but very gentlemanly in his manners. He asked me a great many questions, and I told him one lie, which I have often thought of since. In reply to his query whether Morgan was reinforced before the battle, I told him, "he was not, but that he expected a reinforcement every minute." He asked me how many dragoons Washington had. I replied that "he had seventy, and two volunteer companies of mounted militia—but you know how they won't fight." "By G-d!" he quickly replied, "they did today, though!" I begged him to parole me, but he said, if he did, I should go right off and turn to fighting again. I told him he could get three men in exchange for me, and he replied, "Very well, when we get to Cornwallis' army, you shall be paroled or exchanged; and meanwhile, I'll see that your wounds are taken care of."

We got to Hamilton Ford, on Broad River, about dark. Just before we came to the river, a British dragoon came up at full speed, and told Col. Tarlton that Washington was close behind in pursuit. It was now very dark, and the river was said to be swimming. The British were not willing to take water. Col. Tarlton flew into a terrible passion, and drawing his sword, swore he would cut down the first man who hesitated. They knew him too well to hesitate longer. During the confusion, a young Virginian by the name of Deshaser (also a prisoner) and myself, managed to get into the woods. In truth a

British soldier had agreed to let us escape, and to desert if we would assist him in securing the plunder he had taken.

We slipped away one at a time up the river, Deshaser first, then myself. I waited what I thought a very long time for the British soldier, and he came not. At last I began to think the British were across, and I gave a low whistle—Deshaser answered me, and we met. It was now very dark and raining when we came to the Packolette. I could not find the ford, and it was well, for the river was swimming. We therefore made our way up the river, and had not gone far before we approached a barn. It had a light in it, and I heard a cough. We halted and reconnoitred, and finding it occupied by some British soldiers, we pressed on and soon arrived at old Captain Grant's where I was glad to stop. The old man and his lovely daughter washed and dressed my wounds, and in looking over the bag of plunder which the soldier had given us, they found a fine ruffled shirt, which I put on and went to bed. I shall never forget that girl or the old man for their kindness!

On the next day I left with Deshaser, and arrived at home that evening, where I was confined by a violent fever for eight or ten days; but thanks to the kind nursing and attention of old Mrs. Brandon, I recovered. I now slept in the woods for about three weeks, waiting for some of the whigs to come in and commence operations. I was concerned about a horse. The British soldiers, when they took me, dismounted me from the fine charger I captured at the Cowpens and put me on a pacing pony. One day I met old Molly Willard riding a very fine sorrel horse, and told her we must swap. She wouldn't listen to it—but I replied that there was no use in talking, the horse I would have, and the exchange was made not much to the old woman's satisfaction, for she didn't love the whigs; I don't believe the Willards have forgiven me for that horse swap to this day.

CHAPTER SIX:

From
AUTOBIOGRAPHY OF A
REVOLUTIONARY SOLDIER
by JAMES P. COLLINS*

Like Thomas Youngs' memoir, James Collins Autobiography *is a popular reference for Southern Campaign historians. Writer John Buchanan calls it "a splendid view of a countryside at war as well as the emotions of a boy who became a soldier before his time."†*

Collins's description of Cowpens is neither as anecdotal nor in depth as Young's, yet it does provide several moments of vivid impressionistic imagery. When he writes, "This day I fired my little rifle five times, whether with any effect or not, I do not know," we can imagine a young man from any martial conflict experiencing the same torrid emotions of pride, confusion, terror, and awe in battle.

---

* James Potter Collins, *Autobiography of a Revolutionary Soldier*, John M. Roberts, ed. (Clinton, LA: Feliciana Democrat, 1859).
† John Buchanan, *The Road to Guilford Courthouse: The American Revolution in the Carolinas* (New York: John Wiley & Sons, 1997), 428.

BATTLE OF COWPENS

It was not long until it became necessary for us to seek safety by joining Morgan, who was encamped at the Cowpens, but we were not permitted to remain long idle, for Tarleton came on like a thunder storm, which soon put us to our best mettle. After the tidings of his approach came into camp,—in the night,—we were all awakened, ordered under arms, and formed in order of battle by daybreak. About sunrise on the 17th January, 1781, the enemy came in full view. The sight, to me at least, seemed somewhat imposing; they halted for a short time, and then advanced rapidly, as if certain of victory. The militia under Pickins and Moffitt,* was posted on the right of the regulars some distance in advance, while Washington's cavalry was stationed in the rear. We gave the enemy one fire, when they charged us with their bayonets; we gave way and retreated for our horses, Tarleton's cavalry pursued us; ("now," thought I, "my hide is in the loft;") just as we got to our horses, they overtook us and began to make a few hacks at some, however, without doing much injury. They, in their haste, had pretty much scattered, perhaps, thinking they would have another Fishing creek frolic,† but in a few moments, Col. Washington's cavalry was among them, like a whirlwind, and the poor fellows began to keel from their horses, without being able to remount. The shock was so sudden and violent, they could not stand it, and immediately betook themselves to flight; there was no time to rally, and they appeared to be as hard to stop as a drove of wild Choctaw steers, going to a Pennsylvania market.

---

* Although a Patriot militia company under John Moffett did fight at Cowpens, Collins is most likely referring to Major Joseph McDowell, who commanded North Carolina militia on the right side of the forward skirmish line.

† Fishing Creek was a battle that occurred on August 18, 1780, between British forces under the command of Banastre Tarleton and American forces under Thomas Sumter. Tarleton surprised and routed the American camp, killing or wounding 150 and capturing the one hundred Maryland Continentals dispatched to Sumter by Continental General Horatio Gates prior to Gates's disastrous defeat at Camden on August 16.

BATTLE OF COWPENS

In a few moments the clashing of swords was out of hearing and quickly out of sight; by this time, both lines of the infantry were warmly engaged and we being relieved from the pursuit of the enemy began to rally and prepare to redeem our credit, when Morgan rode up in front, and waving his sword, cried out, "Form, form, my brave fellows! Give them one more fire and the day is ours. Old Morgan was never beaten." We then advanced briskly, and gained the right flank of the enemy, and they being hard pressed in front, by Howard, and falling very fast, could not stand it long. They began to throw down their arms, and surrender themselves prisoners of war. The whole army, except Tarleton and his horsemen, fell into the hands of Morgan, together with all the baggage. After the fight was over, the sight was truly melancholy. The dead on the side of the British, exceeded the number killed at the battle of King's Mountain, being if I recollect aright, three hundred,[*] or upwards. The loss, on the side of the Americans, was only fifteen or sixteen, and a few slightly wounded. This day, I fired my little rifle five times, whether with any effect or not, I do not know. Next day after receiving some small share of the plunder, and taking care to get as much powder as we could, we (the militia) were disbanded and returned to our old haunts, where we obtained a few day's rest.

---

[*] British casualties at Cowpens were 110 dead and two hundred wounded.

CHAPTER SEVEN:

SAMUEL HAMMOND'S "NOTES" ON THE BATTLE OF COWPENS*

Samuel Hammond was a Revolutionary War soldier and officer who fought in many major engagements of the American Revolution. Born in Richmond County, Virginia, he was made a captain of Virginia militia in 1775, then matriculated into the Continental Army. During the early stages of the war, he fought in Virginia, Pennsylvania, and New Jersey. In 1779 he moved to South Carolina, where he joined the Continental Army under General Benjamin Lincoln and raised a regiment of mounted state troops, serving with a dual commission from the state of South Carolina. He served in most of the major engagements of the Southern Campaign, including Savannah, Musgrove's Mill, King's Mountain, Augusta, Ninety Six, and Eutaw Springs.†

At Cowpens, Hammond was assigned command of South Carolina State Troops on the left (or eastern) wing of the skirmish line. According

---

* From *Traditions and Reminiscences, Chiefly of the American Revolution in the South* by Joseph Johnson (Charleston, SC: Walker & James, 1851).
† Lyman G. Draper, *King's Mountain and Its Heroes: History of the Battle of King's Mountain and the Events Which Led To It* (Cincinnati, OH: Peter G. Thomson, Publisher), 467.

to Hammond's pension application, the State Troops who possessed swords and pistols were assigned to Washington's cavalry; those without served under him on the skirmish line. This was in addition to the approximately forty-five militia members, including Thomas Young, who served as mounted dragoons during the battle.*

Hammond's Revolutionary War memoir is both important and problematic. Allegedly collected by his son from Hammond's original notes, the nineteenth-century historian Lyman Draper discounted it for its many inaccuracies. In his account of Cowpens, printed below, he employs a north-to-south orientation, reversing the "left" and "right" orientations employed by most historians. Historian Lawrence Babits suggests this is because the notes were actually written for his men prior to the battle, not for posterity. Babits believes other inconsistencies relate to the position of the different regiments on the field as they camped for the night, not necessarily how they were ultimately aligned for the battle.† Nevertheless, it is widely regarded as the only recordation of Morgan's operation order for Cowpens.‡

On the evening of the 16th January, 1781, General Morgan encamped near a place called the Cowpens. The author of these remarks, being then out with a detachment, did not join the camp until 8 o'clock in the evening, when he was informed by the general, that he intended to give the enemy battle the next morning, if he should press upon him. The ground on which the troops were placed, was a small ridge, nearly parallel with this, lay between three hundred and five hundred yards in his rear. The valley between was made by a gentle slope; it was, of course, brought within range of the eye; passing from one to the other ridge, the land was thickly covered with red oak and hickory, with little if any underbrush. The valleys extending to the right of the general's camp, terminated in a small glade or savanna.

---

* Lawrence E Babits, *A Devil of a Whipping*, 28 and 174 (note 98).
† Ibid, 69.
‡ Lt. Col. John Moncure, *The Cowpens Staff Ride and Battlefield Tour* (Ft. Leavenworth, KS: Combat Studies Institute, 1996), 131.

Orders had been issued to the militia, to have twenty-four rounds of balls prepared and ready for use, before they retired to rest. A general order, forming the disposition of the troops, in case of coming to action, had also been prepared, and was read to Colonels Pickens and McCall, Major Jackson, and the author of these notes, in the course of the evening. No copy was ever afforded to either of these officers, before the battle, and the author of these notes has never since seen them, but in the course of the same evening he made the following notes upon them, then fresh in his memory, and which was shown to Major Jackson and Colonel McCall, and approved by them as correct as far as they went. To show those concerned what would be their stations, the author drew out a rough sketch of the disposition set forth in the general order, and after the action, the rough sketch of the enemy's position was added. No perfect or accurate sketch of the enemy's position was ever drawn; this was only taken by the eye, not by mathematical instruments; and yet no opportunity has been afforded of correcting it. Nevertheless, this gives you a still better idea of the affair, than could be obtained without it.

The order commenced in the substance thus:

As the enemy seemed resolved to force us into action, the numbers and spirit of this little band of patriot soldiers seems to justify the general in the belief they may be met with confidence, defeated and driven back. To prepare for which, the following order will be observed:

The front line will be composed of that part of the Colonel McCall's regiment of South-Carolina State troops, who have not been equipped as dragoons, under the command of Major Hammond; the Georgia volunteers, commanded by Lieutenant-Colonel Cunningham, and the North-Carolina volunteers, under the command of Major McDowal [Joseph McDowell]. Colonel Cunningham will take post on the right, Major McDowal on the left of the line, south-west of the road, upon the rising ground beyond the valley in front, three hundred to three hundred and fifty yards in rear of this cantonment or camp, with the left resting upon the road.

Major Hammond will take post on the left of the road, in line with Colonel Cunningham; supported upon the left by Captain Donoly,* of the Georgia refugees.

The second line will be composed of the continental line of Maryland troops, commanded by Lieutenant-Colonel Howard; on the left of the second line, falling back one hundred yards in its rear, a continuation of the second line, or third line, will be formed, advancing its left wing towards the enemy, so as to bring it nearly parallel with the left of the continental troops, upon the second line. The Virginia militia, commanded by Major Triplet, with the South-Carolina militia, commanded by Captain Beaty, will form to the right of the second line; the left nearly opposite to the right of the second line, one hundred yards in it rear; the right extending towards the enemy, so as to be opposite to or parallel with the second line. The main guard will hold its present position, and be commanded as a present by Colonel Washington's cavalry, with such of Colonel McCall's regiment of new raised South-Carolina State troops, as have been equipped for dragoons, will be a reserve, and form in the rear of Colonel Pickens, beyond the ridge, one or two hundred yards, and nearly opposite the main guard, north of the road.

This is not meant as a correct report of the general order, but as nearly so as the memory, influenced by such events, could be expected to retain.

---

* Captain Donoly, or Donolly, remains unidentified by historians.

CHAPTER EIGHT:

From
A HISTORY OF THE CAMPAIGNS OF 1780 AND 1781, IN THE SOUTHERN PROVINCES OF NORTH AMERICA[*]
by BANASTRE TARLETON

Like many on both the American and British side, Banastre Tarleton published his memoirs after the war. Though the book has earned a place as a valuable reference about the Southern Campaign, particularly for its inclusion of correspondence and other documents, it also has a reputation as being self-serving and unreliable when it comes to Tarleton's losses, as at Cowpens. Its criticisms of Charles Cornwallis played a role in the feud between Cornwallis and the British commander-in-chief in America Henry Clinton that emerged after the war. British officer Roderick Mackenzie, who served under Tarleton at Cowpens, where he was

---

[*] Banastre Tarleton, *A History of the Southern Campaigns of 1780 and 1781, in the Southern Provinces of North American* (London: Printed for T. Cadell, 1787).

wounded, was so incensed by its portrayal he wrote a lengthy rebuttal to the book, a portion of which is included in the next section of this volume.

Though his History *gained some notoriety at the time, Tarleton's glory days were behind him after the American Revolution. He did eventually rise to the rank of general and served several terms in Parliament, but today he is little remembered in England, though in America he remains a convenient villain of the Revolution, occasionally portrayed in movies as the stereotype of a sneering and vindictive British officer. His account here includes several mischaracterizations, which the editor has attempted to point out in footnotes, but is nevertheless included as a primary and unique perspective of one of the battle's major figures.*

During the preparations for the second invasion of North Carolina, emissaries had been dispatched into that province, to obtain intelligence of the force and designs of the Americans. Near the end of December information was received, that General Greene had made a division of his troops, who did not exceed one thousand four hundred men, exclusive of the militia; and, that he had committed the light infantry and Colonel Washington's cavalry to General Morgan, with directions to pass the Catawba and Broad rivers, in order to collect the militia in the districts through which he marched, and afterwards threaten Ninety Six;* whilst he conducted the other division of the continentals to Haley's ferry, on the river Pedee, to form a junction with General Caswell, and give jealousy to Camden. This appeared to be the outline of the American designs previous to the arrival of General Leslie's reinforcement. The intelligence General Greene had procured since his appointment to the southward, and the calculation of his own and the British force, might suggest the propriety of attempting to distress the frontier of South Carolina by a

---

* As Nathanael Greene's letter to Daniel Morgan of December 16, 1781, indicates, Morgan's objective was not to attack Ninety Six, as the British believed.

desultory war, till he could acquire a command sufficiently numerous and well disciplined to undertake more decisive operations. There could not be an arrangement better chosen, provided the royalists were not joined by any additional regiments; but the increase of the English army would certainly frustrate such a disposition. It is not to be supposed that General Greene would have adopted the hazardous plan of dividing and advancing his troops, if he had received authentic information of General Leslie's command being withdrawn from Virginia, and united to the force in South Carolina; because such an accession of strength would naturally produce a movement from Wynnsborough, which, if executed with tolerable rapidity, might separate the two divisions of the American army, and endanger their being totally dispersed or destroyed.*

Whilst the reinforcement marched from Charles town to join the royal forces, Earl Cornwallis employed various measures, in order to acquire daily intelligence of the enemy, and to obtain a competent knowledge of the nature of the country in his front. No expence was spared to learn the state of the roads, the number of the mills, and the quantities of forage and provisions, between Broad river and the Catawba. This information was peculiarly necessary for a general who was about to invade a province not remarkable for its fertility, and which has no navigable rivers to convey supplies to the interior parts of the country.

Tryon county† presented an entrance into North Carolina, which accorded equally with the designs of Earl Cornwallis and the present position of the King's troops. Its comparative abundance, and the proofs of attachment exhibited by the inhabitants, enhanced its local recommendation. The motives

---

* See the editor's "Introduction" about the arrival of Leslie and its influence on Greene's plans.
† Formed in 1768 and named for William Tryon, the colonial governor at the time, Tryon County comprised the southern portion of North Carolina stretching west of the Catawba River from Mecklenburg County.

for the second invasion of North Carolina may be explained in a few words. The strength of the royal army in South Carolina, near the end of the year 1780, allowed Earl Cornwallis the experiment of an enterprize, which the loyalists and British troops in America, as well as the administration in England, supposed he could with facility accomplish. The superiority of his force, when compared with General Greene's, gave every reasonable assurance, that with proper care the latter might be destroyed, or driven over the Roanoke; when it was imagined that the loyalists, who were computed to be the greater proportion of the inhabitants, would make indefatigable exertions to render themselves independent of Congress. Such was the opinion of thousands when the King's troops prepared for this expedition: But their expectations were not verified, though the continental army was chased out of the province, and the loyal subjects were invited to repair to the King's standard at Hillsborough; it therefore becomes necessary to investigate, whether the scheme itself was visionary, or the plan to complete it injudicious; or whether the force employed was inadequate to the purpose.

Earl Cornwallis was not equally sanguine in his expectation of final conquest, it must, however, be universally acknowledged, that the present was a favourable crisis for exertion. The strength of the King's troops, and the weakness of the enemy, strongly recommended this second invasion of North Carolina. On the junction of General Leslie, three thousand five hundred fighting men could advance into that province, besides leaving a large force on the frontier. Any advantage gained over the Americans at this period, would undoubtedly derange their projects, and give a better barrier to South Carolina and Georgia; and though the expedition was ultimately productive only of the advantage of securing old positions, yet the attempting greater objects was justifiable, and gave a fair trial to the ardent wishes of government at home, and the confident hopes of the loyalists in America.

General Leslie, with one thousand five hundred and thirty men, was greatly advanced on his march toward the army, when the operations of the Americans to the westward of Broad river laid immediate claim to the attention of the British. General Morgan, with the continental light infantry, Colonel Washington's cavalry, and large detachments of militia, was reported to be advancing to Ninety Six. Although the fortifications were in tolerable condition at that place, and sufficiently strong to resist an assault, yet the preservation of the country in its neighborhood was considered so great an object for the garrison and the loyalists of the district, that Earl Cornwallis dispatched an aid-de-camp on the 1st of January to order Lieutenant-Colonel Tarleton over Broad river, with the corps of cavalry and infantry, of five hundred and fifty men, the first battalion of the 71st, consisting of two hundred, and two three-pounders,* to counteract the designs of General Morgan, by protecting the country, and compelling him to repass Broad river. Tarleton received a letter the next day from his lordship, communicating an earnest wish, that the American commander, if within his reach, should be "pushed to" the utmost; and requiring, likewise, his opinion, whether any move of the main army would be advantageous the service.† On the receipt of this letter, he directed his course to the westward, and employed every engine to obtain intelligence of the enemy. He had not proceeded above twenty miles from Brierley's ferry, before he had undoubted proofs, that the report which occasioned the order for the light troops to march was erroneous. The secure state of Ninety Six, and the distance of General Morgan, immediately prompted Tarleton to halt the troops under his command, as well to allow time for the junction of the baggage of the different corps, which had been left on the ground when they first decamped, as to give information to Earl Cornwallis of the situation and force of

---

* The "three-pounder" was a light field artillery piece that fired a projectile weighing approximately three pounds. Nicknamed the "Grasshopper," it was typically mounted on wheels and could be pulled by a horse, making it useful for expeditionary forces like Tarleton's.
† See Cornwallis's letter to Tarleton of January 2, 1781.

Morgan, and to propose operations which required his sanction and concurrence.

As Lieutenant-colonel Tarleton had been entrusted with the outline of the future campaign, he thought it incumbent on him to lay before his lordship, by letter, the probable accounts of Morgan's force and designs; the necessity of waiting for the baggage of the light troops in their present situation, as any future delay might prove a great inconvenience to the army; and the plan of operation which struck him as equally necessary and advantageous for the King's service. He represented the course to be taken, which fortunately corresponded with the scheme of the campaign: He mentioned the mode of proceeding to be employed against General Morgan: He proposed the same time, for the army and the light troops to commence their march: He explained the point to be attained by the main body: And he declared, that it should be his endeavour to push the enemy into that quarter.*

Earl Cornwallis approving the suggested operations, the light troops only waited for their baggage to proceed. Two hundred men of the 7th regiment, who were chiefly recruits, and designed for the garrison at Ninety Six, and fifty dragoons of the 17th regiment, brought the waggons from Brierley's to camp. On their arrival, Lieutenant-colonel Tarleton crossed Indian, and afterwards Dunken creek, though both were considerably swelled by a late fall of rain: He hourly received accounts of the increase of Morgan's corps, which induced him to request Earl Cornwallis, who was moving on the east of the Broad river, to give him permission to retain the 7th regiment, that the enemy might be sooner passed over Broad river, or some favourable situation obtained, whence great advantage might be derived from additional numbers: Having received leave to carry forwards the 7th regiment, he continued his course on the 12th to the westward, in order to discover the

---

* See Tarleton's letter of January 4, 1781, and Cornwallis's reply of January 5.

most practicable fords for the passage of the Ennoree and Tyger, and that the infantry might avoid the inconveniencies they had undergone in crossing the other waters. An useful expedient was concealed under this apparent necessity. In proportion to the approach of the light troops to the sources of the rivers, and the progress of the main army to King's mountain, General Morgan's danger would increase, if he remained to the westward of Broad river. The Ennoree and Tyger were passed on the 14th, above the Cherokee road, and Tarleton obtained information in the evening that General Morgan guarded all the fords upon the Pacolet. About the same time Earl Cornwallis advertised Tarleton, that the main army had reached Bull's run, and that General Leslie had surmounted the difficulties which had hitherto retarded his march. At this crisis Lieutenant-colonel Tarleton assured Earl Cornwallis that he would endeavour to pass the Pacolet, purposely to force General Morgan to retreat towards Broad river, and requested his lordship to proceed up the eastern bank without delay, because such a movement might perhaps admit of cooperation, and would undoubtedly stop the retreat of the Americans.*

On the 15th circumstantial intelligence was procured by Lieutenant-colonel Tarleton of the different guards stationed on the Pacolet. A march was commenced in the evening towards the iron works, which are situated high upon the river; but in the morning the course was altered and the light troops secured a passage within six miles of the enemy's camp. As soon as the corps were assembled beyond the Pacolet, Lieutenant-colonel Tarleton thought it advisable to advance towards some log houses, formerly constructed by Major Ferguson, which lay midway between the British and

---

* No existing record of this correspondence exists. Tarleton may be referring to his letters of January 9 and January 11, which Cornwallis references in his correspondence but have not been preserved. Cornwallis did not move in conjunction with Tarleton, allowing Morgan to escape across the Broad River after the battle.

Americans, and were reported to be unoccupied by General Morgan. The necessity and utility of such a proceeding appeared so strong, that some dragoons and mounted infantry were sent with all possible expedition to secure them, lest a similar opinion should strike the American commander, which might be productive of great inconvenience. Tarleton intended to take post, with his whole corps, behind the log house, and wait the motions of the enemy; but a patrole discovering that the Americans were decamped, the British light troops were directed to occupy their position, because it yielded a good post, and afforded plenty of provisions, which they had left behind them, half cooked, in every part of their encampment.

Patroles and spies were immediately dispatched to observe the Americans: The dragoons were directed to follow the enemy till dark, and the other emissaries to continue their inquiries till morning, if some material incident did not occur: Early in the night the patroles reported that General Morgan had struck into byways, tending towards Thickelle creek:* A party of determined loyalists made an American colonel prisoner, who had casually left the line of march, and conducted him to the British camp: The examination of the militia colonel, and other accounts soon afterwards received, evinced the propriety of hanging upon General Morgan's rear, to impede the junction of reinforcements, said to be approaching, and likewise to prevent his passing Broad river without the knowledge of the light troops, who could perplex his design, and call in the assistance of the main army if necessity required. Other reports at midnight of a corps of mountaineers being upon the march from Green river, proved the exigency of moving to watch the enemy closely, in order to take advantage of any favourable opportunity that might offer.†

---

* Thicketty Creek in what is now western Cherokee County, South Carolina, running near the Cowpens battlefield.

† This may be a reference to militia regiments from the mountainous region of what is now Burke County, North Carolina, who joined Morgan before the battle.

Accordingly, at three o'clock in the morning on the 17th, the pickets being called in, the British troops, under the command of Lieutenant-colonel Tarleton, were directed to follow the route the Americans had taken the preceding evening, and the baggage and waggons were ordered to remain upon their ground till daybreak, under the protection of a detachment from each corps. Three companies of light infantry, supported by the legion infantry, formed the advance: the 7th regiment, the guns, and the 1st battalion of the 71st, composed the center; and the cavalry and mounted infantry brought up the rear. The ground which the Americans had passed being broken, and much intersected by creeks and ravines, the march of the British troops during the darkness was exceedingly slow, on account of the time employed in examining the front and flanks as they proceeded. Before dawn, Thickelle creek was passed, when an advanced guard of cavalry was ordered to the front. The enemy's patrole approaching, was pursued and overtaken: Two troops of dragoons, under Captain Ogilvie, of the legion, were then ordered to reinforce the advanced guard, and to harass the rear of the enemy. The march had not continued long in this manner, before the commanding officer in front reported that the American troops were halted and forming. The guides were immediately consulted relative to the ground which General Morgan then occupied, and the country in his rear. These people described both with great perspicuity: They said that the woods were open and free from swamps; that the part of Broad river, just above the place where King's creek joined the stream, was about six miles distant from the enemy's left flank, and that the river, by making a curve to the westward, ran parallel to their rear.

Lieutenant-colonel Tarleton having attained a position, which he certainly might deem advantageous, on account of the vulnerable situation of the enemy, and the supposed vicinity of the two British corps on the east and west of Broad river, did not hesitate to undertake those measures which the instructions of his commanding officer imposed, and his own judgement, under the present appearances, equally recommended. He ordered the legion dragoons to drive in the militia parties who covered the front, that General Morgan's disposition might be conveniently and distinctly inspected.

He discovered that the American commander had formed a front line of about one thousand militia, and had composed his second line and reserve of five hundred continental light infantry, one hundred and twenty of Washington's cavalry, and three hundred back woodsmen.* This accurate knowledge being obtained, Tarleton desired the British infantry to disencumber themselves of every thing, except their arms and ammunition: The light infantry were then ordered to file to the right till they became equal to the flank of the American front line: The legion infantry were added to their left; and, under the fire of a three-pounder, this part of the British troops was instructed to advance within three hundred yards of the enemy. This situation being acquired, the 7th regiment was commanded to form upon the left of the legion infantry, and the other three-pounder was given to the right division of the 7th: A captain, with fifty dragoons, was placed on each flank of the corps, who formed the British front line, to protect their own, and threaten the flanks of the enemy: The 1st battalion of the 71st was desired to extend a little to the left of the 7th regiment, and to remain one hundred and fifty yards in the rear. This body of infantry, and near two hundred cavalry, composed the reserve. During the execution of these arrangements, the animation of the officer & and the alacrity of the soldiers afforded the most promising assurances of success. The disposition being completed, the front line received orders to advance; a fire from some of the recruits of the 7th regiment was suppressed, and the troops moved on in as good a line as

---

* Tarleton grossly exaggerates the number of Patriot militia at Cowpens. Historian Christopher Ward calculates Morgan's total force at approximately 1,050, including six hundred Continental soldiers and the rest Patriot militia. He calculates Morgan's forward skirmish line at approximately 150 men.

troops could move at open files:* The militia, after a short contest, were dislodged, and the British approached the continentals. The fire on both sides was well supported, and produced much slaughter: The cavalry on the right were directed to charge the enemy's left: They executed the order with great gallantry, but were drove back by the fire of the reserve, and by a charge of Colonel Washington's cavalry.

As the contest between the British infantry in the front line and the continentals seemed equally balanced, neither retreating, Lieutenant-colonel Tarleton thought the advance of the 71st into line, and a movement of the cavalry in reserve to threaten the enemy's right flank, would put a victorious period to the action. No time was lost in performing this maneuver. The 71st were desired to pass the 7th before they gave their fire, and were directed not to entangle their right flank with the left of the other battalion. The cavalry were ordered to incline to the left, and to form a line, which would embrace the whole of the enemy's right flank. Upon the advance of the 71st, all the infantry again moved on: The continentals and back woodsmen gave ground: The British rushed forwards: An order was dispatched to the cavalry to charge: An unexpected fire at this instant from the Americans, who came about as they were retreating, stopped the British, and threw them into confusion. Exertions to make them advance were useless. The part of the cavalry which had not been engaged fell likewise into disorder, and an unaccountable panic extended itself along the whole line. The Americans, who before thought they had lost the action, taking advantage of the present situation, advanced upon the British troops, and augmented their astonishment. A general flight ensued. Tarleton sent directions to his cavalry to form about four hundred yards to the right of the enemy, in order to check them, whilst he endeavoured to rally the infantry to protect the guns. The cavalry did not comply with the order, and the effort to collect the infantry

---

* Tarleton was later criticized for ordering his main line to advance before they were properly formed. See the editor's "Introduction."

was ineffectual: Neither promises nor threats could gain their attention; they surrendered or dispersed, and abandoned the guns to the artillery men, who defended them for some time with exemplary resolution. In this last stage of defeat Lieutenant-colonel Tarleton made another struggle to bring his cavalry to the charge. The weight of such an attack might yet retrieve the day, the enemy being much broken by their late rapid advance; but all attempts to restore order, recollection, or courage, proved fruitless. Above two hundred dragoons forsook their leader, and left the field of battle. Fourteen officers and forty horse men were, however, not unmindful of their own reputation, or the situation of their commanding officer. Colonel Washington's cavalry were charged, and driven back into the continental infantry by this handful of brave men. Another party of the Americans, who had seized upon the baggage of the British troops on the road from the late encampment, were dispersed, and this detachment retired towards Broad river unmolested. On the route Tarleton heard with infinite grief and astonishment, that the main army had not advanced beyond Turkey creek: He therefore directed his course to the south east, in order to reach Hamilton's ford, near the mouth of Bullock creek, whence he might communicate with Earl Cornwallis.

The number of the killed and wounded, in the action at the Cowpens, amounted to near three hundred on both sides, officers and men inclusive[*]: This loss was almost equally shared; but the Americans took two pieces of cannon, the colours[†] of the 7th regiment, and near four hundred prisoners.

---

[*] Not surprisingly, Tarleton overestimates American casualties.
[†] Colours, or regimental flags, were used in battle to enhance organization and mark the location of the commander but more symbolically represented the esteem and tradition of the regiment. To have them captured in battle, therefore, was an insult to the regiment's honor.

CHAPTER NINE:

From
STRICTURES ON LT. COL. TARLETON'S HISTORY "OF THE CAMPAIGNS OF 1780 AND 1781, IN THE SOUTHERN PROVINCES OF NORTH AMERICA"... IN A SERIES OF LETTERS TO A FRIEND[*]
by RODERICK MACKENZIE

Roderick Mackenzie was an officer in the British 71st Regiment who was wounded at Cowpens. Roderick, it appears, shared an opinion of Tarleton with his commanding officer, Major Archibald McArthur, who after the battle told Continental Lieutenant Colonel John Eager Howard the best troops in the British service had been put under command of "that boy," Banastre Tarleton, "to be sacrificed."[†]

---

[*] Roderick Mackenzie, *Strictures on Lt. Col. Tarleton's History "of The Campaigns of 1780 and 1781, in the Southern Provinces of North America"... In a Series of Letters to a Friend* (London: 1787).

[†] This account of John Eager Howard appears in a footnote in *The Campaign of 1781 in the Carolinas* by Henry Lee.

After the war, Mackenzie was incensed by Banastre Tarleton's A History of the Campaigns in 1780 and 1781, *published in 1787, in particular its many criticisms of Cornwallis. Later that same year, he published his own rebuttal, excerpted here. Written as a "Series of Letters to a Friend," and dedicated to Francis, Lord Rawdon, the book is a caustic and often brutal takedown, with particular attention paid to what he believed were Tarleton's many mistakes at Cowpens. As such, it is far from an objective account. Still, Mackenzie was a notable eyewitness to the events from the British side, and his commentary appears in numerous histories of the battle.*

This chapter has been abridged.

From Letter IX

I now proceed to examine the account which our author has given to the world of his defeat at Cowpens, but previous to this investigation it will be necessary to inquire, what degree of credit is due to this description of the advance to the field of battle. The traits of self-importance which it contains are too apparent to escape the notice of any reader.

Lieutenant Colonel Tarleton landed in American in the year 1777, with the rank of Cornet of Dragoons, and in the beginning of January, 1781, we find him the primum mobile, the master spring which puts the whole machinery of the army in motion. It is a received maxim to listen with caution to the hero of his own story; but we are naturally prepossessed in favor of those who speak modestly of themselves, and honourably of others; my present object, however, is to consider how far our author has followed the lines which he declares himself to have prescribed.

He says, page 220, "The distance between Wynnsborough and Little Broad River, which would have answered the same propose, does not exceed fifty-five miles: Earl Cornwallis commenced his march on the 7th or 8th of January. It would be mortifying to describe the advantages that might have resulted from his Lordship's arrival at the concerted point, or to expatiate upon calamities which were produced by this event."

The imputed censures in the above paragraph demand a dispassionate investigation. Let us admit, that the possession of King's Mountain was a point preconcerted between Earl Cornwallis and Lieutenant Colonel Tarleton; it shall also be granted, that the attainment of the eminence by the main body, was a measure well calculated to cut off Morgan's retreat; neither is it meant to be denied that Lieutenant Colonel Tarleton used means to overtake the American detachment which do him no discredit: but granting all that, it is contended, that the rapidity of his movements did not afford Earl Cornwallis time to arrive at the point above-mentioned; and it shall be demonstrated, that an allowance of additional time for that arrival, was entirely in the power of our author; and farther, that it would have attended with many conspicuous advantages.

His mode of reasoning, in the present instance, is invidious in the extreme, with respect to the General, and is equally contemptuous of the judgment of every officer in his army: it is a bold stroke of imposition even upon the common sense of mankind: because it will be readily granted, by every person, that a march of fifty-five miles may easily be made out in the course of ten days, he, therefore, eagerly takes advantage of that obvious fact, to support his uniform drift, of attempting to render the General reprehensible. And as his Lordship commenced his march on the 7th or 8th, if difficulties and obstacles, which our author artfully conceals, had not intervened, he might certainly have arrived at the place of destination by the 17th. But let us take a candid and impartial review of this matter, and it will clearly appear, that this censurer of his General's conduct had no right to expect the arrival of the army at King's Mountain, by the time which he specifies.

We have his own testimony of his having received due information that the army on the 14th had not got farther than Bull Run. This then is the point, both with respect to time and distance, from which we are to estimate the movements of the main body, as well as of the detachment; and hence are we to fix the criterion from which we are to derive our judgment of the subsequent conduct of both commanders.

The distance of Bull run, where the General was on the 14th, from King's Mountain, is forty-five miles. Our author's position at the same period of time, was not more remote from the spot of his precipitate engagement with the enemy than thirty miles. This engagement took place on the morning of the 17th, before one hour of daylight had passed. Instead therefore of an allowance of ten days, for a march of fifty-five miles, we now find, in fact, the General had only two days to perform a march of forty-five miles; and it is but bare justices to point out the many obstacles which the army, on this occasion, had to surmount. Both the ground through which his Lordship had to pass, and the weather, opposed all possibility of a quick progress. Every step of his march was obstructed by creeks and rivulets, all of which were swelled to a prodigious height, and many rendered quite unfordable, in consequence of a heavy fall of rain for several weeks; to these difficulties were also added, the encumbrance of a train of artillery, military stores, baggage, and all the other necessary appointments of an army. On the other hand, our author had only to lead on about a thousand light troops, in the best condition, and as little encumbered as possible; with these, as I can assuredly attest, by swimming horses and felling trees for bridges, means which were impracticable to his Lordship's army, he came up with the enemy much sooner than was expected.

I have now laid before you a simple and fair statement of the advance, as well as of the army as of the detachment, previous to the unfortunate action at Cowpens, and furnished you with a clue by which you may unravel the windings and doublings of our author.

The real province of an historian is to relate facts; by this principle he should abide; whenever he deviates from it, and indulges a fanciful vein of conjecture concerning probable contingencies, if not totally divested of partiality, he is certain of misleading his readers.

Of all men, Lieutenant Colonel Tarleton should be the last to censure Earl Cornwallis for not destroying Morgan's force; as it will appear that the provision made for that service was perfectly sufficient; and though it can by no means be admitted that his Lordship could have maneuvered so as to get General Green into his power after the defeat at Cowpens; it may, however, be affirmed, that if the troops lost on that occasion had escaped the misfortune that befell them, and had been combined with the British force at the battle of Guilford, the victory must have been more decisive.

I will hazard an additional reflection: Had Earl Cornwallis not been deprived of his light troops, the blockade at York Town had never taken place; and the enemies of our country would have sued for peace.

From Letter X

The defeat of the British detachment at Cowpens, which I informed you would be the subject of this letter, has been variously represented by different authors; it is a point, however, in which they all agree, that at a particular stage of the engagement the whole American infantry gave way, and, that the legion-cavalry, though three times the number of those of the enemy, contributed noting to complete their confusion.

I was upon the detachment in question, and the narrative which I now offer has been submitted to the judgment of several respectable officers, who were also in this action, and it has met with their entire approbation.

Toward the latter end of December 1780, Lieutenant Colonel Tarleton was detached with the light and legion infantry, the fusiliers, the first battalion of the 71st regiment, about three hundred fifty cavalry, two field-pieces, and an adequate proportion of men from the royal artillery; in all near a thousand strong. This corps, after a progress of some days, arrived at the vicinity of Ninety Six, a post which was then commanded by Lieutenant Colonel Allen. An offer of reinforcement was made to Lieutenant Colonel Tarleton. The offers was rejected; and the detachment, by fatiguing marches, attained the ground which Morgan had quitted a few hours before: This position was taken about ten o'clock on the evening of the 16th of January. The pursuit re-commenced by two o'clock the next morning, and was rapidly continued through marshes and broken grounds till day-light, when the enemy were discovered in front. Two of their videttes were taken soon after; these gave information that General Morgan had halted, and prepared for action; he had formed his troops in an open wood, secured neither in front, flank, nor rear. Without the delay of a single moment, and in despite of extreme fatigue, the light-legion infantry and fusiliers were ordered to form in line. Before this order was put in execution, and while Major Newmarsh, who commanded the latter corps, was posting his officers, the line, far from complete, was led to the attack by Lieutenant Colonel Tarleton himself. The seventy-first regiment and cavalry, who had not as yet disentangled themselves from the brushwood with which Thickette Creek abounds, were directed to form, and wait for orders.

  The military valour of British troops when not entirely divested of the powers necessary to its exertion was not to be resisted by an American militia. They gave way on all quarters, and were pursued to their continentals; the second line, now attacked, made a stout resistance. Captain Ogilvie, with his troop, which did not exceed forty men, was ordered to charge the right flank of the enemy. He cut his way through their line, but exposed to a heavy fire, and charged at the same time by the whole of Washington's dragoons, was compelled to retreat in confusion. The reserve, which as yet had no orders to move from its first position, and consequently remained near a mile distant was now directed to advance. When the line felt "the advance of the seventy-first, all the infantry again moved on: the continentals and backwoods-men gave ground: the British rushed forwards: an order was dispatched to the cavalry to charge."* This order, however, if such was then thought of, being either not delivered or disobeyed, they stood aloof, without availing themselves of the fairest opportunity of reaping the laurels which lay before them.

The infantry were not in condition to overtake the fugitives; the latter had not marched thirty miles in the course of the last fortnight; the former, during that time, had been in motion day and night. A number, not less than two-thirds of the British infantry officers, had already fallen, and nearly the same proportion of privates; fatigue, however, enfeebled the pursuit, much more than loss of blood. Morgan soon discovered that the legion-cavalry did not advance, and that the infantry, though well disposed, were unable to come up with his corps: he ordered Colonel Washington, with his dragoons, to cover his retreat, and check the pursuit. He was obeyed; and the protection thus afforded, gave him an opportunity of rallying his scattered forces. They formed, renewed the attack, and charged in their turn. In disorder from the pursuit, unsupported by the cavalry, deprived of the assistance of the cannon, which in defiance of the utmost exertions of those who had them in charge, were now left behind, the advance of the British fell back, and communicated a panick to others, which soon became general: a total rout ensued.

Two hundred and fifty horse which had not been engaged, fled through the woods with the utmost precipitation, bearing down such officers as opposed their flight; the cannon were soon seized by the Americans, the detachment from the train being either killed or wounded in their defence; and the infantry were easily overtaken, as the cause which had retarded the pursuit, had now and equal effect in impeding the retreat: dispirited on many accounts, they surrendered at discretion. Even at this late stage of the defeat, Lieutenant Colonel Tarleton, with no more than fifty horse, hesitated not to charge the whole of Washington's cavalry, though supported by the

---

* This quote is from Banastre Tarleton's *History of the Campaigns of 1780 and 1781*, page 217.

Continentals; it was a small body officers, and a detachment of the seventeenth regiment of dragoons, who presented themselves on this desperate occasion; the loss sustained was in proportion to the danger of the enterprise, and the whole was repulsed.

A detachment from each corps, under the command of Lieutenant Fraser of the 71st regiment (who was afterwards killed at York Town), had been left at some distance to guard the baggage; early intelligence of the defeat was conveyed to this officer by some friendly Americans; what part of the baggage could not be carried off he immediately destroyed, and with his men mounted on the wagon, and spare horses, he retreated to Earl Cornwallis unmolested; nor did he, on this occasion see any of the American horse or foot, or of the party then under our author's* discretions. This was the only body of infantry that escaped, the rest were either killed or made prisoners. The dragoons joined the army in two separate divisions; one arrived in the neighbourhood of the British encampment on the evening of the same day, at which his Lordship had the mortification to learn the defeat of the detachment; the other, under Lieutenant Colonel Tarleton, appeared next morning.

From Letter XI

As a circumstantial detail of the action at Cowpens was given to you in my last letter, observations upon the causes of that disaster shall be the subject of this.

As an individual on this detachment, credit may be given to me for an acquaintance with every circumstance which is here described. If to be disinterested is necessary for investigation of truth, I come so far qualified for this task. Unconnected with party, devoid of spleen, and too unimportant to be affected by general reflections on collective

---

* The word "author" is a reference to Tarleton.

bounties of military men, candour and impartiality maybe be allowed me—But to proceed.

The first error in judgment to be imputed to Lieutenant Colonel Tarleton, on the morning of the 17th of January, 1781, is, the not halting his troops before engaging the enemy. Had he done so, it was evident that the following advantages would have been the result of his conduct. General Morgan's force and situation might have been distinctly viewed, under cover of a very superior cavalry; the British infantry, fatigued with rapid marches, day and night, for some time past, as has already been observed, might have had rest and refreshment; a detachment from the several corps left with the baggage, together with batt-men, and officers servants, would have had time to come up, and join in the action. The artillery all this time might have been playing on the enemy's front, or either flank, without risk of insult; the commandants of regiments, Majors McArthur and Newmarsh, officers who held commissions long before our author was born, and who had reputations to this day unimpeached, might have been consulted, and, not to dwell on the enumeration of the advantages which would have accrued from so judicious a delay, time would have been given for the approach of Earl Cornwallis to the preconcerted point, for the unattainment of which he has been so much and so unjustly censured.

The second error was, the un-officer-like impetuosity of directing the line to advance before it was properly formed, and before the reserve had taken its ground; in consequence of which, as might have been expected, the attack was premature, confused, and irregular.

The third error in this ruinous business, was the omission of giving discretional power to that judicious veteran McArthur, to advance with the reserve, at the time the front line was in pursuit of the militia, by which means the connection so necessary to troops in the field was not preserved.

His fourth error was, ordering Captain Ogilvie, with a troop, consisting of no more than forty men, to charge, before any impression was made of the continentals, and before Washington's cavalry had been engaged.

The next, and the most destructive, for I will not pretend to follow him through all his errors, was in not bringing up a column of cavalry, and completing the rout, which, by his own acknowledgment, had commenced through the whole American infantry.

After what has been said, there may not, perhaps, be a better criterion to judge of the conduct of those corps, upon whom Lieutenant Colonel Tarleton has stamped the charge of "total misbehaviour," than by an examination of the state of discipline they were then under, of their general conduct upon former occasion, and of the loss which they sustained on this.

The fusiliers had served with credit in American from the commencement of the war, and under an excellent officer, General Clarke, had attained the summit of military discipline: they had at this time, out of nine officers who were in the action, five killed and wounded.

Killed:	Captain Heylar
	Lieutenant Marshal
	Major Newmarsh
Wounded:	Lieutenant Harling
	Lieutenant L'Estrange

The first battalion of the 71st regiment, who had landed in Georgia in the year 1778, under the command of Sir Archibald Campbell, had established their reputation in the several operations in that province, at Stono Ferry, at the sieges of Savannah and Charlestown, and at the battle of Camden. Now, not inferior to the 7th regiment in discipline, they were led by an officer of great experience, who had come into the British service from the Scotch Dutch brigade: Out of sixteen officers, which they had in the field, nine were killed and wounded.

BATTLE OF COWPENS

Light companies of the 1st and 2nd 71st included:

Killed:	Lieutenant Macleod
	Lieutenant Chisholm
Wounded:	Lieutenant Grant
	Lieutenant Mackintosh
	Lieutenant Flint
	Lieutenant Mackenzie
	Lieutenant Sinclair
	Lieutenant Forbes
	Lieutenant Macleod

The battalion of the light infantry had signalised themselves separately on many occasions. The company of the 16th regiment was well known by its services in the army command by Major General Prevost; those of the seventy-first regiment were distinguished under Sir James Baird at the surprise of General Wayne in Pennsylvania, of Baylor's dragoons in New Jersey, at Briar Creek in Georgia, at the capture and subsequent defence of Savannah, at the battle near Camden under Earl Cornwallis; and even Lieutenant Colonel Tarleton did them justice at the defeat of Sumpter, just after the last mentioned action.*

The light infantry company was of the Prince of Wales's American regiment, when but newly raised and indifferently disciplined, acquired reputation under General Tryon at Danbury; their only officer was here wounded.

The infantry and legion had seen much service, and had always behaved well: this our author will surely not deny.

The troops of the seventeenth regiment of dragoons, when ordered into action, displayed that gallantry with which

---

* This is a reference to the Battle of Fishing Creek on August 18, 1780, where Tarleton surprised and defeated a mixed force of Patriot militia and Continental soldiers under command of South Carolina partisan Thomas Sumter, killing many and recapturing British supply convoys Sumter had captured the day before.

they had stamped their character on every former occasion. They had here but two officers, both of whom were wounded, one mortally. The detachment of artillery was totally annihilated.

Such were the troops whom this journalist has so severely stigmatized. Few corps, in any age or country, will be found to have bled more freely.

It is an established custom in armies for the commanding officer, whether victorious or vanquished, to account for the loss which he has sustained. In the present instance it requires no extraordinary sagacity to discover, that Lieutenant Colonel Tarleton had his own particular reasons for withholding such an account; and it is evident that had this loss of officers, to which that of the soldiers probably bore a near proportion, been faithfully published, the veracity of our author's account might have been justly called into question.

I have now done with the action at Cowpens, and on this occasion confess that I am not without my feelings as an individual for so wanton an attack on characters and entire corps, whose conduct had been, till then, unsullied. There is not an officer who survived that disastrous day, who is not far beyond the reach of slander and detraction; and with respect to the dead, I leave Lieutenant Colonel Tarleton all the satisfaction which he can enjoy, from reflecting that he led a number of brave men to destruction, and then used every effort in his power to damn their fame with posterity.

CHAPTER TEN:

DANIEL MORGAN'S REPORT ON THE BATTLE OF COWPENS*

Written as a letter to Nathanael Greene, Daniel Morgan's account of Cowpens is a model of military efficiency, especially given the reams written about the battle since. Though it may lack the context of those other accounts, it succinctly outlines the major salient points: Morgan's movement prior to the battle; his reasons for fighting at Cowpens; the famous disposition of his troops in three lines, with militia stationed on the forward two; the orchestration of the battle; and its glorious results (at least from the American persepective). "Such was the inferiority of our numbers

---

* "Daniel Morgan to Nathanael Greene," January 19, 1781, from *Cowpens Papers: Being Correspondence of General Morgan and the Prominent Actors*, Theodorus Bailey Myers, ed. (Charleston, SC: The News & Courier, 1881). Paragraph breaks have been added to facilitate the modern reader.

that our success must be attributed, under God, to the justice of our cause and the bravery of our Troops," Morgan writes with eloquence, equating the great American cause with one of our great American battlefield victories. Nobody could've written it better.

January 19th, 1781

DEAR SIR—The troops I have the honor to command have gained a complete victory over a detachment from the British Army commanded by Lieut.-Col. Tarleton. It happened on the 17th inst., about sunrise, at a place called the Cowpens, near Pacolet River. On the 14th, having received intelligence that the British Army were in motion, and that their movements clearly indicated the intention of dislodging me, I abandoned my encampment at Glendale Ford,* and on the 16th, in the evening, took possession of a post about seven miles from Chroke on Broad River. My former position subjected me at once to the operations of Lord Cornwallis and Colonel Tarleton, and in case of a defeat my retreat might easily have been cut off. My situation at Cowpens enabled me to improve any advantage that I might gain and to provide better for my security should I be unfortunate. These reasons induced me to take this post, notwithstanding it had the appearance of a retreat. On the evening of the 16th, the enemy occupied the ground we had removed from in the morning. One hour before daylight one of my scouts informed me that they had advanced within five miles of our camp. On this information the necessary dispositions were made. From the activity of the troops we soon prepared to receive them. The light infantry commanded by Lt.-Col. Howard, and the Virginia Militia under Major Triplett, were formed on a rising ground. The Third Regiment of Dragoons consisting of about 80 men, under command of Lt. Col. Washington, were so posted in the rear

---

* A misstatement. Morgan's camp was at Grindal (or Grindle) Shoals on the Pacolet River. Another modern spelling is Grindall Shoals.

as not to be injured by the enemy's fire, and yet to be able to charge them should an occasion offer; the Volunteers from North Carolina, South Carolina and Georgia under the command of Col. Pickens were posted to guard the flanks. Major McDowal,* of the North Carolina Volunteers, were posted on the right flank in front of the line 150 yards. Major Cunningham, of the Georgia Volunteers, on the left, at the same distance in front, Colonels Brannon and Thomas, of the South Carolina Volunteers, on the right of Major McDowal, and Colonels Hays and McCall of the same corps to the left of Major Cunningham. Capts. Tate and Buchanan, with the Augusta Riflemen, were to support the right of the line.

The enemy drew up in one line four hundred yards in front of our advanced corps. The first battalion of the 71st Regiment was opposed to our right, the 7th to our left, the Legion Infantry to our centre, and two companies of the light troops, 100 each, on our flanks. In their front they moved two pieces of artillery, and Lieut.-Col. Tarleton, with 280 cavalry, was posted in the rear of the line. The disposition being thus made, small parties of riflemen were detached to skirmish with the enemy, on which the whole line advanced with the greatest impetuosity, shouting as they advanced. Majors McDowal and Cunningham gave them a heavy and galling fire, and retreated to the regiments intended for their support; the whole of Col. Pickens' command then kept up a fire by regiments, retreating agreeable to orders. When the enemy advanced on our lines they received a well directed and incessant fire, but their numbers being superior to ours they gained our flanks, which obliged us to change our position. We retired, in good order, about fifty paces, formed and advanced on the enemy and gave them a brisk fire, which threw them into disorder. Lieut.-Col. Howard observing this gave orders for the line to charge bayonets, which was done with such address that the enemy

---

* This is a reference to Joseph McDowell, a North Carolina militia leader from what is now Burke County, North Carolina.

fled with the utmost precipitation. Lieut.-Col. Washington discovering that the cavalry were cutting down our riflemen on the left, charged them with such firmness as obliged them to retire in confusion.

The enemy were entirely routed, and the pursuit continued upwards of twenty miles. Our loss was inconsiderable, not having more than twelve killed and sixty wounded. The enemy's loss was 10 commissioned officers and over 100 rank and file killed and 200 wounded, 29 commissioned officers and about 500 privates prisoners which fell into our hands with two pieces of artillery, two standards, 800 muskets, one travelling forge, thirty-five baggage wagons, seventy negroes and upwards of 100 dragoon horses, with all their musick. They destroyed most of the baggage which was immense. Although our success was complete we fought only 800 men and were opposed by upwards of one thousand chosen British Troops.* Such was the inferiority of our numbers that our success must be attributed, under God, to the justice of our cause and the bravery of our Troops. My wishes would induce me to mention the name of every private centinel in the Corps. In justice to the brave and good conduct of the officers, I have taken the liberty to enclose you a list of their names from a conviction that you will be pleased to introduce such characters to the world. Major Giles, my aid de camp, and Captain Brooks, acting as Brigade Major, deserve to have my thanks for their assistance and behavior on this occasion. The Baron de Glabuck, who accompanies Major Giles with these despatches, behaved in such manner as to merit your attention.

I am sir, Your obedient servant,
DAN MORGAN

---

*Modern scholarship places the number of Morgan's men at approximately 1,050. As he had militia joining him throughout the night, Morgan is forgiven for slightly underreporting his strength.

Part Four: Analysis & Contemporary Accounts

CHAPTER ELEVEN:

From
THE ACCOUNT OF CHARLES, LORD CORNWALLIS, TO HENRY CLINTON*

In contrast to the succinct eloquence of Daniel Morgan, who had good reason to embellish the account of his astonishing victory, Cornwallis's concise report to his superior officer, Henry Clinton, is perhaps more understandable: Nobody likes to give the boss bad news.

Nevertheless, Cornwallis lays out a logical argument supporting the motives for the British action: with Cornwallis ready to commence his campaign into North Carolina, strategy dictated that he drive Morgan from his rear; the force that he dispatched against Morgan under Tarleton was superior in quality and artillery; and the enemy's position in an open field favored Tarleton's cavalry. "Every thing now bore the most promising aspect," he writes.

---

* From Banastre Tarleton's *A History of the Southern Campaigns of 1780 and 1781, in the Southern Provinces of North American* (London: Printed for T. Cadell, 1787).

But then things turned horribly wrong. Like many an executive before or since explaining the failure of a strategic initiative under his or her authority, Cornwallis lays the blame on an incomprehensible twist of fate. The enemy's unexpected turn caused the "utmost confusion," as occasionally occurs in the chaos of war.

Clinton wasn't buying it. "We have here, unfortunately, another fatal instance of the ruinous effect of risking detachments without being in a situation to sustain them, or [of] promising and not affording support," he wrote caustically in his memoir of the war.* But the real rub between Clinton and Cornwallis is hinted at in the next to last paragraph, where Cornwallis assures Clinton, "Your excellency may be assured that nothing but the most absolute necessity shall induce me to give up the important object of the winter's campaign." After the war, Cornwallis's insistence on initiating the invasion of North Carolina, despite the disaster at Cowpens, would play a role in a bitter feud between the two British generals over who was to blame for losing the American Revolution, with Clinton asserting Cornwallis should've stayed put in South Carolina, and Cornwallis countering that the only way to win the South was to subdue North Carolina and Virginia.

January 18th, 1781

SIR—In my letter of the 6th of this month I had the honour to inform your excellency, that I was ready to begin my march for North Carolina, having been delayed some days by a diversion made by the enemy towards Ninety Six. General Morgan still remained on the Pacolet; his corps, by the best accounts I could get, consisted of about five hundred men, continental and Virginia state troops, and one hundred cavalry under Colonel Washington, and six or seven hundred militia: But that body is so fluctuating that is impossible to ascertain its number, within some hundreds for three days following.

---

* Henry Clinton, *The American Rebellion: Sir Henry Clinton's Narrative of His Campaigns, 1775-1782* (New Haven, CT: Yale University Press, 1954), 247.

BATTLE OF COWPENS

Lieutenant-colonel Tarleton, with the legion, and corps annexed to it, consisting of about three hundred cavalry, and as many infantry, and the 1st battalion of the 71st regiment, and one three-pounder had already passed the Broad river for the relief of Ninety Six. I therefore directed Lieutenant-colonel Tarleton to march on the west of Broad river, to endeavour to strike a blow at General Morgan, and at all events to oblige him to repass the Broad river; I likewise ordered that he should take with him the 7th regiment and one three-pounder, which were marching to reinforce the garrison of Ninety Six, as long as he should think their services could be useful to him. The remainder of the army marched between the Broad river and Catawba.*

As General Greene had quitted Mecklenburgh county, and crossed the Pedee, I made not the least doubt that General Morgan would retire on our advancing. The progress of the army was greatly impeded by heavy rains, which swelled the rivers and creeks; yet Lieutenant-colonel Tarleton conducted his march so well, and got so near to General Morgan, who was retreating before him, as to make it dangerous for him to pass Broad river, and came up with him at eight o'clock of the morning of the 17th instant. Every thing now bore the most promising aspect: The enemy were drawn up in an open wood, and, having been lately joined by some militia, were more numerous; but the different quality of the corps under Lieutenant-colonel Tarleton's command, and his great superiority in cavalry, left him no room to doubt of the most brilliant success. The attack was begun by the first line of infantry, consisting of the 7th regiment, the infantry of the legion, and corps of light infantry annexed to it; a troop of cavalry was placed on each flank; the 1st battalion of the 71st, and the remainder of the cavalry, formed the reserve. The enemy's line soon gave way, and their militia quitted the field;

---

* Cornwallis's broad generalization misrepresents his army's lack of progress.

but our troops having been thrown into some disorder by the pursuit, General Morgan's corps faced about, and gave them a heavy fire: This unexpected event occasioned the utmost confusion in the first line: The 1st battalion of the 71st, and the cavalry, were successfully ordered up; but neither the exertions, entreaties, or example, of Lieutenant-colonel Tarleton, could prevent the panic from becoming general. The two three-pounders were taken, and, I fear, the colours of the 7th regiment shared the same fate. In justice to the detachment of the royal artillery, I must here observe, that no terror could induce them to abandon their guns, and they were all either killed or wounded in the defence of them. Lieutenant-colonel Tarleton with difficulty assembled fifty of his cavalry, who, having had time to recollect themselves; and being animated with the bravery of the officer who had so often led them to victory, charged and repulsed Colonel Washington's horse, retook the baggage of the corps, and cut to pieces the detachment of the enemy who had taken possession of it; and after destroying what they could not conveniently bring off, retired with the remainder, unmolested, to Hamilton's ford, near the mouth of Bullock's creek. The loss of our cavalry is inconsiderable; but I fear about four hundred of the infantry are either killed, wounded, or taken. I will transmit the particular account of the loss as soon as it can be ascertained.

It is impossible to foresee all the consequences that this unexpected and extraordinary event may produce; but your excellency may be assured that nothing but the most absolute necessity shall induce me to give up the important object of the winter's campaign.[*]

I have the honour to be, &c.

CORNWALLIS

---

[*] See the "Introduction" for more on British plans for the winter campaign and invasion of North Carolina.

CHAPTER TWELVE:

From
MEMOIRS OF THE WAR IN THE SOUTHERN DEPARTMENT OF THE UNITED STATES*
By HENRY LEE

Though Henry Lee's memoir of the American Revolution wasn't published until 1812, it remains a valuable account of the Southern Campaign. The son of a prominent Virginia family, Lee joined the Continental Army shortly after graduating from Princeton and quickly rose through the ranks, thanks in part to the horsemanship that earned him his nickname, "Light Horse Harry," not to mention the patronage of his fellow Virginian George Washington. Hand selected by Nathanael Greene to serve in the Southern Army, Lee was not actually at Cowpens (rather, he was fighting with famed South Carolina militia general Francis "Swamp Fox" Marion in eastern South Carolina at the time), leading to the occasional inaccuracy in his account. Nevertheless, Lee

---

* From Henry Lee, *Memoirs of the War in the Southern Department of the United States* (Washington, DC: Peter Force, 1827) *served with many of the officers and soldiers at Cowpens and would've heard many firsthand narratives of the battle.*

Lee's account is valuable mostly for its cogent criticisms of both Morgan and Tarleton. Having not been at the battle, Lee could not have known the many contingencies faced by these leaders, yet his analysis is strategically sound. In particular, he dissects the many mistakes made by Tarleton.

After the war, Lee served as governor of Virginia but struggled with debt and bad investments. Written as an attempt to stave off his creditors, his memoir has become a beloved historic resource, its occasional hyperbole tolerated in exchange for its many enduring anecdotes and vigorous prose style. Lee's memoirs included many footnotes, which have been included here with the heading of "Lee's Footnote" to distinguish them from the editor's.

Soon after Tarleton had been detached in pursuit of Morgan, the British general put his army in motion. Having in view the interception of Morgan, should he elude Tarleton, and preferring to advance into North Carolina on the upper route, to avoid as much as possible the obstructions, usual at that season, from the rising of the water-courses, Cornwallis directed his march between the Catawba and Broad River. To keep in doubt his plan of operations, General Leslie had been continued at Camden; but he was now directed to move on the eastern side of the Wateree and Catawba, parallel to his lordship's route.

Lieutenant-Colonel Tarleton lost no time in approaching his enemy. Morgan was duly apprised of this advance, and of the movement of the British army. At the head of the troops, able and willing to fight, he was rather disposed to meet than to avoid his foe; and would probably have resolved on immediate action, had he not felt the danger of delay in consequence of Cornwallis's advance up the Catawba. Nevertheless, he indicated a desire to dispute the passage of the Pacolet, to which Tarleton was fast approaching; but he relinquished this plan, in consequence of the enemy's having passed the river on his right or above him, and retired with a degree of precipitation which proved how judiciously the British commandant had taken his first steps. Tarleton passed through the ground on which Morgan had been encamped, a few hours after the latter had abandoned it; and leaving his baggage under a guard, with orders to follow with convenient expedition, he passed forward throughout the night in pursuit of the retiring foe.* After a severe march through a rugged country, he came in sign of the enemy about eight o'clock in the morning (January 17, 1781), and having taken two of our vedettes, he learned that Morgan had halted at the Cowpens, not far in front, and some distance from Broad River. Presuming that Morgan would not risk action unless driven to it, Tarleton determined, fatigued as his troops were, instantly to advance on his enemy, lest he might throw his corps safe over Broad River.

Morgan, having been accustomed to fight and to conquer, did not relish the eager and interrupting pursuit of his adversary; and set down at the Cowpens to give refreshment to his troops, with a resolution to no longer avoid action, should his enemy persist in pressing it. Being apprised at the dawn of the day of Tarleton's advance, he instantly prepared for battle. This decision grew out of the irritation of temper, which appears to have overruled the suggestions of his sound and discriminating judgement.† The ground about the Cowpens is covered with open wood, admitting the operation of cavalry

---

* Lee compresses the events of January 15 and 16 into one day. Morgan abandoned his camp on the Pacolet River on January 15; Tarleton passed the Pacolet on January 16.
† Lee's Footnote: On this passage Colonel Howard remarks—that Morgan did not decide on action until he was joined in the night by Pickens and his followers—and adds: "I well remember that parties were coming in most of the night, and calling on Morgan for ammunition, and to know the state of affairs. They were all in good spirits, related circumstances of Tarleton's cruelty, and expressed the strongest desire to check his progress." The probability is, that these circumstances confirmed the decision Morgan had already formed.

with facility, in which the enemy trebled Morgan. His flanks had no resting-place, but were exposed to be readily turned; and Broad River ran parallel to his rear, forbidding the hope of a safe retreat in the event of disaster. Had Morgan crossed the river, and approached the mountain, he would have gained a position disadvantageous to cavalry, but convenient for riflemen, and would have secured a less dangerous retreat. But these cogent reasons, rendered more forcible by his inferiority in numbers, could not prevail.* Confiding in his long-tried fortune, conscious of his personal superiority in soldiership, and relying on the skill and courage of his troops, he adhered to his resolution. Erroneous was the decision to fight in this position, when a better might have been easily gained, the disposition for battle was masterly.

Two light parties of militia, under Major McDowel [Joseph McDowell], of North Carolina, and Major Cunningham, of Georgia, were advanced in front, with orders to feel the enemy as he approached; and, preserving a desultory well-aimed fire as they fell back to the front line, to range with it and renew the conflict. The main body of the militia composed this line, with General Pickens at its head. At a suitable distance in the rear of the first line a second was stationed, composed of the Continental infantry and two companies of Virginia militia, under Captains Triplett and Taite,† command by Lieutenant-Colonel Howard.

---

* Lee's criticisms here ignore other contingencies faced by Morgan: Morgan feared that if he retreated across the Broad his militia would desert him.

† Lee's Footnote: These two companies of militia were generally Continental soldiers, who, having served the time of their enlistment, had returned home regularly discharged.

A custom for some time past prevailed, which gave to us the aid of such soldiers. Voluntary proffer of service being no longer fashionable, the militia were drafted conformably to a system established by law; and whenever the lot fell upon the timid or wealthy, he procured, by a douceur, a substitute, who, for the most part, was one of those heretofore discharged.

Washington's cavalry, re-enforced with a company of mounted militia armed with sabres, was held in reserve, convenient to support the infantry, and protect the horses of the rifle militia, which were tied, agreeably to usage, in the rear. On the verge of battle, Morgan availed himself of the short and awful interim to exhort his troops. First addressing himself, with his characteristic pith, to the line of the militia, he extolled the zeal and bravery so often displayed of them, when unsupported by the bayonet or sword; and declared his confidence that they could not fail in maintaining their reputation, when supported by chose bodies of horse and foot, and conducted by himself. Nor did he forget to glance at his unvarying fortune, and superior experience; or to mention how often, with his corps of riflemen, he had brought British troops, equal to those before him, to submission. He described the deep regret he had already experienced in being obliged, form prudential considerations, to retire before an enemy always in his power; exhorted the line to be firm and steady; to fire with good aim; and if they would pour in but two volleys at killing distance, he would take upon himself to secure victory. To the Continentals he was very brief. He reminded them of the confidence he had always reposed in their skill and courage; assured them the victory was certain if they acted well their part; and desired them not to be discouraged by the sudden retreat of the militia *that* being part of his plan and orders. Then taking post with this line, he waited in stern silence for the enemy.

The British lieutenant-colonel, urging forward, was at length gratified with the certainty of battle; and being prone to presume on victory, he hurried the formation of his troops. The light and Legion infantry, with the seventh regiment, composed the line of battle; in the centre of which was posted the artillery, consisting of two grasshoppers*; and a troop of dragoons was placed on each flank. The battalion of the seventy-first regiment, under Major McArthur, with the

---

* "Grasshoppers" is a pseudonym for "three-pounders," the light artillery that fired a three-pound shot.

remainder of the cavalry, formed the reserve. Tarleton placed himself with the line, having under him Major Newmarsh, who commanded the seventh regiment. The disposition was not completed, when he directed the line to advance, and the reserve to wait for further orders.* The American light parties quickly yielded, fell back, and arrayed with Pickens. The enemy shouting, rushed forward upon the front line, which retained its station, and poured in a close fire; but continuing to advance with the bayonet on our militia, they retired, and gained with haste the second line. Here, with part of the corps, Pickens took post on Howard's right, and the rest fled to their horses; probably with orders to remove them to a further distance. Tarleton pushed forward, and was received by his adversary with unshaken firmness. The contest became obstinate; and each party, animated by the example of its leader, nobly contended for victory. Our line maintained itself so firmly, as to oblige the enemy to order up his reserve. The advance of McArthur re-animated the British line, which again moved forward; and, outstretching our front, endangered Howard's right. The officer instantly took measures to defend his flank, by directing his right company to its front; but mistaking this order, the company fell back; upon which the line began to retire, and General Morgan directed it to retreat to the cavalry. This manoeuvre being peformed with precision, our flank became relieved, and the new position was assumed with promptitude. Considering this retrograde movement the precursor of flight, the British line rushed on with impetuosity and disorder; but, as it drew near, Howard faced about, and gave it a close and murderous fire. Stunned by this unexpected shock, the most advanced of the enemy recoiled in confusion.

---

* Lee's Footnote: Tarleton's cavalry are stated at three hundred and fifty, while that under Morgan did not exceed eighty.
    Morgan's militia used rifles, and were expert marksmen; this corps composed nearly one half of his infantry.
    Tarleton's detachment is put down as one thousand. Morgan in a letter to General Green, after his victory, gives his total as eight hundred.

Howard seized the happy moment, and followed his advantage with the bayonet.* This decisive step gave us the day. The reserve having been brought near the line, shared in the destruction of our fire, and presented no rallying point to the fugitives. A part of the enemy's cavalry, having gained our rear, fell on that portion of the militia who had retired to their horses. Washington struck at them with his dragoons, and drove them before him. Thus, by simultaneous efforts, the infantry and the cavalry of the enemy were routed. Morgan pressed home his success, and the pursuit became vigorous and general. The British cavalry having taken no part in the action, except the two troops attached to the line, were in force to cover the retreat. This, however, was not done. The zeal of Lieutenant-Colonel Washington to pursue having carried him far before his squadron, Tarleton turned upon him the troop of the seventeenth regiment of dragoons, seconded by many of his officers. The American lieutenant-colonel was first rescued from this critical contest by one of his sergeants, and afterwards a fortunate shot from his bugler's pistol.† This check concluded resistance on the part of the British officer, who drew off with the remains of his cavalry, collected his stragglers, and hastened to Lord Cornwallis. The baggage guard, learning the issue of battle, moved instantly toward the

---

* Lee's Footnote: In this charge the brave Kirkwood, of the Delawares, was conspicuous.
† Lee's Footnote: In the eagerness of pursuit, Washington advanced nearly thirty yards in front of his regiment. Observing this, three British officers wheeled about, and made a charge upon him. The officer on his right was aiming to cut him down, when a sergeant came up and intercepted the blow by disabling his sword arm. At the same instant, the officer on his left was about make a stroke at him, when a waiter, too small to wield a sword, saved him by wounding the officer with a ball, discharged from a pistol. At this moment the officer in the centre, who was believed to be Tarleton, made a thrust at him, which he parried; upon which the officer retreated a few paces, and then discharged a pistol at him, which wounded his knee."—MARSHALL'S *Life of Washington*.

British army. A part of the horse, who had shamefully avoided action, and refused to charge when Tarleton wheeled on the impetuous Washington, reached the camp of Cornwallis at Fisher's Creek, about twenty-five miles from the Cowpens, in the evening. The remainder arrived with Lieutenant-Colonel Tarleton on the morning following. In this decisive battle we lost about seventy men, of whom twelve only were killed. The British infantry, with the exception of the baggage guard, were nearly all killed or taken. One hundred, including ten officers were killed; twenty-three officers and five hundred privates were taken. The artillery, eight hundred muskets, two standards, thirty-five baggage wagons, and one hundred dragoon horses, fell into our possession.*

The victory of Cowpens was to the South what that of Bennington† had been to the North. General Morgan, whose former services had placed him high in public estimation, was now deservedly ranked among the most illustrious defenders of his country. Starke fought an inferior, Morgan a superior, foe. The former contended with a German‡ corps; the latter, with the *elite* of the Southern army, composed of British troops. In military reputation the conqueror at the Cowpens must stand before the hero of Bennington. Starke was nobly

---

* Lee's Footnote: Cornwallis's letter to Sir H. Clinton.

† The Battle of Bennington took place on August 16, 1777. American forces under General John Stark defeated a detachment of John Burgoyne's British Army made up mostly of Hessian soldiers. Part of the Saratoga campaign, the battle was a decisive victory for the Americans and is widely considered a turning point in the American Revolution.

‡ Lee's Footnote: This remark is not made to disparage the German troops serving with the British army in America. They were excellent soldiers; but, for light services, they were inferior to the British. Ignorant of our language, unaccustomed to woods, with their very heavy dress, they were less capable of active and quick operations.

The splendid issue of the subsequent campaign, and the triumph of Gates has been noticed, as well as the instrumentality of Morgan in producing the auspicious event. Great and effectual as were his exertions, General Gates did not even mention him in his official dispatch.

seconded by Colonel Warner and his Continental regiment; Morgan derived very great aid from Pickens and his militia, and was effectually supported by Howard and Washington. The weight of the battle fell on Howard; who sustained himself admirably in trying circumstances, and seized with decision the critical moment to complete with the bayonet the advantage gained by his fire.

Congress manifested their sense of this important victory by a resolve, approving the conduct of the principal officers, and commemorative of their distinguished exertions. To General Morgan they presented a gold medal, to Brigadier Pickens a sword, and to Lieutenant-Colonels Howard and Washington a silver medal, and to Captain Triplett a sword.

While all must acknowledge the splendor of this achievement, it must be admitted, that the errors of the British commandant contributed not a little to our signal success. The moment he came in sight of the American detachment, he must have been sure of his first wish and object—battle. Where then was the necessity for that hurry which he took his measures? It was but little after sunrise; and consequently, after giving rest to the fatigued troops, there would have been time enough for the full accomplishment of his views. That interval he might have advantageously employed in a personal examination of his enemy's position, and in disclosure of his plans to his principal officers. He knew well the composition of Morgan's corps, and the American mode of fighting. The front line, being composed of militia, he was well apprised would yield; and that the struggle for victory must take place after he reached our regulars. He ought not to have run upon the retiring militia with his infantry, but should have brought them up in full bodily capacity for the contest. A portion of dragoons might and ought to have borne down on Pickens, when retiring. But instead of that, Tarleton himself, with the first line, pressed forward and fell upon our main body with exhausted breath. The fatigued, panting, disappointed British, as might have been expected, paused. Tarleton instantly called up his reserves, which approached near the line, suffered with it from our fire, and became useless. Here he violated the fundamental rules of battle. The reserve, as the term indicates, ought not to be endangered by the fire levelled at the preceding body; but, being safe from musketry by its distance, should be ready to interpose in case of disaster, and to increase advantage in the event of victory. In his "Campaigns," he acknowledges that the ground was disadvantageous to his adversary, and favorable to himself; speaks of the alacrity with which his troops advanced into action; and admits the leading facts, on which these observations are founded. He could not deny that he had two field-pieces, and Morgan none; that he was vastly superior in cavalry; that his troops were among the best in the British army; and that he rather exceeded his enemy in numbers, whose regulars, horse and foot, were less than five hundred.

These facts admitted, how can the issue of the battle be satisfactorily explained without acknowledging that the British leader did not avail himself of the advantage he possessed; that his improvidence and precipitancy influenced the result, and that General Morgan exhibited a personal superiority in the art of war! This conclusion, however contested by Lieutenant-Colonel Tarleton and his particular friends, will be approved by the enlightened and impartial of both armies; and posterity will confirm the decision.

CHAPTER THIRTEEN:

From
*THE HISTORY OF THE ORIGIN, PROGRESS AND TERMINATION OF THE AMERICAN WAR**
by CHARLES STEDMAN

Charles Stedman was born in Philadelphia in 1753 to a prominent family. After studying law at the College of William and Mary, he joined the British Army as a commissary officer, serving under British commander-in-chief William Howe before joining Cornwallis in the Southern Campaign. After the American Revolution he retired to England on half-pay as a Colonel, publishing his two-volume history of the American Revolution in 1784.†

Though criticized for plagiarizing large portions of the text, Stedman's History *remains a valuable resource, especially of the Southern Campaign, where he was witness to many of its events. Though he was not*

---

* Charles Stedman, *The History of the Origin, Progress, and Termination of the American War*, Volume II (London: printed by the author, 1794).
† Edward W. James, "Charles Stedman," The William and Mary Quarterly, Vol. 8, No. 1 (July, 1899), p. 34.

at Cowpens with Tarleton, he was nearby and would've heard many accounts of the battle from its officers and soldiers. Not surprisingly for a British officer, this account credits the American victory more to luck than the stratagem of Morgan and his officers, but its criticism of Banastre Tarleton is not sparing. Perhaps most significant, however, is the perspective it provides on the battle's historic consequences: "The defeat of his majesty's troops at the Cowpens formed a very principal link in the chain of circumstances which led to the independence of America," he surmises, a view that has stood the test of time.

Paragraph breaks have been added to the text to ehance readability. Spelling and capitalization have been retained from the original text.

Morgan, in his march, had collected about four or five hundred militia, and upon his approach to the district of Ninety-six, was joined by two hundred more, who had fled from the frontiers of Georgia when Augusta was taken possession of by the British troops.[*] Thus the two detachments were nearly equal in point of numbers, but in cavalry, and in general quality of the troops, Tarleton was greatly superior. The British army now proceeded to the north-west, between Broad River and the Catawba. This route, leading to the back country, was chosen, that the army might the more easily be enable to pass the great rivers in its way at the ford's near their source: It also afforded a prospect of cutting off Morgan's retreat, if he should elude Tarleton, or at least of preventing his junction with the army under general Greene: Nor was the British general without hopes that by following this course he might get between Greene's army and Virginia, and force him to an action before he was joined by his expected reinforcements.

The detachment under general Leslie, which had been purposely halted at Camden, until lord Cornwallis should be ready to march from Wynnesborough, the longer to conceal from the American general the road which the British army

---

[*] The strength of Morgan's militia fluctuated broadly in the weeks, days, and hours leading up to the battle.

meant to take, now received orders to move up the banks of the Catawba, and join the main army on its march. The march of both Lord Cornwallis and general Leslie, encumbered as they were with baggage and artillery, was greatly retarded by the swelling creeks and water-courses. These obstacles Tarleton also experienced; but having command of light troops, he more easily surmounted them, and probably overtook Morgan something sooner than was expected.

The latter, after retreating over the Pacolet, made a show of disputing Tarleton's passage by guarding the fords. Tarleton, however, on the 9th of January, found means to pass over his detachment within six miles of the enemy's encampment; and Morgan was obliged to make a precipitate retreat, leaving in his camp the provisions that were dressing for his troops half cooked. Tarleton advanced and took possession of the ground that had been left by the enemy only a few hours before.*

At three in the morning the march of the British light troops was resumed in pursuit of general Morgan; the baggage being left under a guard composed of a detachment from each corps with orders not to move till daylight appeared. Tarleton, after a fatiguing march through swamps and broken grounds, at length came in sight of the enemy about eight in the morning; Two of their videttes were soon afterwards taken; and from them information was received that the Americans had halted, and were forming at a place called the Cowpens.†

General Morgan, finding himself hard pressed by the British troops, had resolved to hazard an action rather than be overtaken in the ford of the river. With this view he drew up his force in two lines, the militia under colonel Pickens forming the first line, and the continentals, under colonel Howard with the Virginia rifle-men, the second. Washington's dragoons, with some mounted militia, were drawn up at some

---

* An inaccuracy. Tarleton crossed the Pacolet River on the morning of January 16, 1781.
† Tarleton's own account states he had discovered this information earlier in the night.

BATTLE OF COWPENS

distance in the rear, as a corps of reserve. The ground which occupied does not appear to have been well chosen: It was an open wood, and consequently liable to be penetrated by the British cavalry: Both his flanks were exposed; and the river, at no great distance, ran parallel to his rear. In such a situation he gave a manifest advantage to the enemy with a superior body of cavalry; and in case of a defeat, the destruction of his whole detachment was inevitable.

Lieutenant-colonel Tarleton, upon receiving the intelligence communicated by the videttes, resolved, without loss of time, to make an attack upon the Americans. Advancing within two hundred and fifty yards of their first line, he made a hasty disposition of his force. The light and legion infantry, and the seventh regiment, were ordered to form in line, a captain, with fifty dragoons, being attached to each of their flanks; and the first battalion of the seventy-first regiment, and the rest of the cavalry, were directed to form as a reserve, and wait for orders.

This disposition being settled, Tarleton, relying on the valour of this troops, impatient of delay, and too confident of success, led on in person the first line to the attack, even before it was fully formed, and whilst major Newmarsh, who commanded the seventh regiment, was posting his officers; Neither had the reserve yet reached the ground which it was to occupy. The first line of the Americans being composed of militia, did not long withstand the charge of the British regulars: It gave way in all quarters and was pursued to the continentals. The latter, undismayed by the retreat of the militia, maintained their ground with great bravery: and the conflict between them and the British troops was obstinate and bloody. Captain Ogilvie, with his troop of dragoons on the right of the British line, was directed to charge the left Bank of the enemy. He cut his way through their line, but being exposed to a heavy fire, and, at the same time, charged by the whole of Washington's cavalry, was compelled to retreat in confusion.

The British reserve now received orders to move forward; and as soon as the line felt the advance of the seventy-first regiment, the whole again moved on. The continentals, no longer able to stand the shock, were forced to give way. This was the critical moment of the action, which might have been improved so as to secure to the British troops a complete victory. An order, it is said, was dispatched to the cavalry to charge the enemy when in confusion; but if such an order was delivered, it was not obeyed; and the infantry, enfeebled by their fatiguing march in the morning, through swamps and broken grounds, and by their subsequent exertions in the action, were unable to come up with the flying enemy.

The critical moment lost on one side was eagerly seized on the other. The American commander, finding that the British cavalry did not pursue, gave orders to Washington to cover with his dragoons the rear of the broken provincials, whilst he exerted himself to the utmost to rally them. His endeavours succeeded: The continentals were rallied and formed, and now in their turn charged the assailants. In disorder from the pursuit, and unsupported by the cavalry, such of the British infantry as were farthest advanced, receiving this unexpected charge, fell back in confusion, and communicated a panic to others, which soon became general. Washington charged with his cavalry; and a total rout ensued. The militia who had fled, seeing the fortune of the day changed, returned and joined in the pursuit. The British infantry were soon overtaken, as the same causes which retarded them in the pursuit, now impeded their flight; and almost the whole were either killed or taken prisoners. The two field-pieces were also taken, but not till the whole of the artillery-men attached to them were either killed or wounded.

It was in vain that Tarleton endeavoured to bring his legion cavalry to charge and check the progress of the enemy: They still stood aloof, and at length fled in a body through the woods, leaving their commander behind. Fourteen officers, however, remained with him, and about forty men of the seventeenth regiment of dragoons: At the head of these he made a desperate charge on the whole of Washington's cavalry, and drove them back upon the continentals. But no partial advantage, however brilliant, could now retrieve the fortune of the day: All was already lost; and Tarleton, seeing nothing farther to be done, retreated with the remains of this small but brave and faithful band of adherents, to Hamilton's Ford, upon Broad River, on his way to the main army under Lord Cornwallis, then at Turkey Creek, about twenty-five miles from the field of action. The only body of Tarleton's infantry that escaped was the guard left behind with the baggage, which had not reached the Cowpens at the time of the action: Early intelligence of the defeat being conveyed to the officer who commanded it, by some friendly Americans, he immediately destroyed whatever part of the baggage could not be carried off, and mounting his men on the waggon and spare horses, retreated to the main army unmolested.

Few of the legion cavalry were missing: One division of them arrived the same evening in the neighbourhood of the British encampment, with the news of their defeat, and another under Tarleton, who in his way had been joined by some stragglers, appeared the next morning. The whole loss of the British troops, in this unfortunate affair, amounted to at least six hundred men; and of them near one half was either killed or wounded. The loss of the Americans, according to their report of it, was so small as scarcely to deserve credit. It amounted to twelve killed, and sixty wounded.

During the whole period of the war no other action reflected so much dishonour upon the British arms. The British were superior in numbers. Morgan had only five hundred and forty continentals, the rest militia. Tarleton's force composed the light troops of lord Cornwallis's army. Every disaster that befell lord Cornwallis, after Tarleton's most shameful defeat at the Cowpens, may most justly be attributed to the imprudence and unsoldierly conduct of that officer in the action. It was asked, why he did not consult the majors McArthur and Newmarsh, officers of experience and reputation, who had been in service before Tarleton was born?

Colonel Tarleton, in his *History of the Southern Campaigns in America*, admits that the ground on which Morgan formed had been described with great perspicuity to him. He also admits, that he had obtained a very accurate knowledge of Morgan's situation, and of the ground on which Morgan had drawn up his army. That there was every prospect of success from the animation and alacrity of his troops; that his troops moved in a good line; that his fire was well supported, and produced much slaughter; that the continentals and back woodsmen gave ground, and the British rushed forward; that the ground Morgan had chosen was disadvantageous for the Americans, and as proper a situation for action as colonel Tarleton could have wished: Under all these advantages in favour of Tarleton, and disadvantages against Morgan, Tarleton is completely defeated and routed.

Is it possible for the mind to form any other conclusion, than that there was a radical defect, and a want of military knowledge on the part of colonel Tarleton? That he possesses personal bravery inferior to no man, is beyond a doubt; but his talents at the period we are speaking of never exceeded that of a partisan captain of light dragoons, daring in skirmishes. He could defeat an enemy in detail, by continually harassing, and cutting off detached parties.

The defeat of his majesty's troops at the Cowpens formed a very principal link in the chain of circumstances which led to the independence of America. Colonel Tarleton acquired power without any extraordinary degree of merit, and upon most occasions exercised it without discretion.

Nothing could be more unexpected by lord Cornwallis, than the news of Tarleton's discomfiture. If he judged from the events of former actions, where the numbers were not so equally balanced, and the disproportion much more in favour of the Americans, he had reason to look for a victory instead of a defeat. The disappointment was galling: and the loss of credit cast a shade over the commencement of the expedition. But another consequence of the defeat was of a still more serious nature: The loss of the light troops, at all times necessary to an army, but on a march through a woody and thinly settled country, almost indispensable, was not to be repaired.

CHAPTER FOURTEEN:

From
THE HISTORY OF THE REVOLUTION OF SOUTH CAROLINA, FROM A BRITISH PROVINCE TO AN INDEPENDENT STATE, VOLUME TWO[*]
by DAVID RAMSAY, M.D., member of the AMERICAN CONGRESS

David Ramsay was one of the earliest historians of the American Revolution. Born in Maryland, he had been educated at Princeton and trained as a physician in Philadelphia before moving to Charleston, South Carolina, in 1774 to practice his craft. He served in the South Carolina legislature during the American Revolution until he was captured by the British. After the war, he served two terms in the Continental Congress, from 1782 to 1783 and again from 1785 to 1786. This work, his

---

[*] David Ramsay, *The History of the Revolution of South Carolina, from a British Province to an Independent State*, Volume II (Trenton, NJ: Isaac Collins, 1785).

History of the Revolution of South Carolina, *was his earliest, published in two volumes in 1785. Later he would go on to publish several more historical works, including the landmark* History of the American Revolution *in 1789, a broader study of the war.*

As a member of the South Carolina legislature, Ramsay personally knew many of the war's key figures in the colony, including Thomas Sumter and Francis Marion. However, for his history of Cowpens, he would have relied on second- or third-hand accounts. Therefore, this is a relatively brief portrait of the important battle, compressing key events and misreporting some of the results. For instance, Ramsay reports the Americans took five hundred British prisoners, exclusive of the wounded, when the number is now widely acknowledged to be six hundred. It is more significant in its description of the political influences shaping the allegiances of the South Carolina back country in the months and weeks leading up to the battle (though one must account for Ramsay's Whig sympathies), as well as for its prescient assessment of the battle's lasting impact. As one of the first commercially published accounts of the American Revolution, particularly its events in the South, Ramsay's history would have been the first opportunity many Americans had to read about the battle aside from newspaper accounts. You are reading it here as those early Americans would have read it then. This edit includes a few minor spelling corrections of proper names and some added paragraph breaks.

After the general submission of the militia in the year 1780, a revolution took place highly favourable to the interests of America. The residence of the British army, instead of increasing the real friends to royal government, diminished their number, and added new vigour to the opposite party. In the district of Ninety-Six, moderate measures were at first adopted by the British commanders, but the effects of this were frustrated by the royalists. A great part of those who called themselves the King's friends, had been at all times a banditti, to whom rapine and violence were familiar. On the restoration of royal government, these men preferred their claim to its particular notice. The conquerors were so far imposed on them, that they promoted some of them who were of the most infamous characters. Men of such base minds and mercenary principles, regardless of the capitulation, gratified their private resentments, and their rage for plunder, to the great distress of the newmade subjects, and the greater injury of the royal interest. Violence of this kind made some men break their engagements to the British, and join the Americans. Their revolt occasioned suspicions to the prejudice of others who had no intention of following their example. Fears, jealousies, and distrust, haunted the minds of the conquerors. All confidence was an end.

Severe measures were next tried, but with a worse effect. Lieutenant-colonel Balfour, an haughty and imperious officer, who commanded in that district, was more calculated, by his insolence and overbearing conduct, to alienate the inhabitants from a government already beloved, than to reconcile them to one which was generally dislike. By an unwarrantable stretch of his authority, he issued a proclamation, by which it was declared, "that every man who was not in his house by a certain day, should be subject to military execution." The British had a post in Ninety-Six for thirteen months, during which the country was filled with rapine, violence, and murder. Applications were made daily for redress, yet in that whole period there was not a single instance wherein punishment was inflicted either on the soldiery or tories. The people soon found that there was no security for their lives, liberties or property, under the military government of British officers, which subjected them to the depredations of a malicious mercenary banditti, falsely calling themselves the friends of royal government.

The peaceable citizens were reduced to that uncommon distress, in which they had more to fear from oppression than resistance; they therefore most ardently wished for the appearance of an American force. Under these favourable circumstances general Greene detached general Morgan to take a position in the western extremity of the state. There he arrived on the twenty-fifth of December 1780. On the twenty-ninth he dispatched lieutenant-colonel Washington, with his own regiment, and two hundred militia-horse, commanded by lieutenant-colonel McCall, to attack a body of tories who were plundering the whig inhabitants. Lieutenant-colonel Washington came up with them on the thirtieth, near Hammond's storehouse, and charged them, on which they all fled without making any resistance. Many were killed or wounded, and about forty taken prisoners.*

On the next day lieutenant-colonel Washington detached cornet James Simons, with a command of elven regulars and twenty-five militia, to pursue the fugitives, and to surprize a fort a few miles distant, in which general Cunningham† commanded about one hundred and fifty British militia. This fort,‡ situated seventeen miles from Ninety-Six, was strongly pickquetted in every direction; and, besides containing a great deal of plunder taken from the whig inhabitants, was well stored with forage, grain, and other provisions for the use of the British army. As soon as the Americans were discovered, general Cunningham and all his men abounded the fort. Cornet Simons stationed his detachment, and advancing with a flag, demanded their surrender. General Cunningham requested time to consult with his officers, and five minutes were given him for that purpose. In that short space the whole party of tories ran off, and dispersed themselves through the woods. Cornet Simons, after destroying the fort, and all the provisions in it, which he could not carry away, rejoined lieutenant-colonel Washington without molestation.

---

* See the editor's introduction for more on the engagement at Hammond's Store. Daniel Morgan would report to Nathanael Greene that 150 Loyalists were killed there, without a single Patriot loss, leading some historians to suggest the encounter was more slaughter than battle.

† Robert Cunningham was a prominent Loyalist community leader and politician in the South Carolina back country. On November 22, 1780, he was appointed Brigadier General of the Loyalist militia in the Ninety Six District by General Cornwallis.

‡ A reference to "Williams Fort" or "Fort Williams"; see footnote on page 40 for more about Williams Fort.

These successes, the appearance of the American army, a sincere attachment to the cause of independence, and the impolitick conduct of the British, induced several persons to resume their arms, and to act in concert with the detachment of continentals. Lord Cornwallis wished to drive general Morgan from his station, and to deter the inhabitants from joining him. Lieutenant-colonel Tarleton, at the head of a thousand regulars, was ordered to execute this business. The British had two field-pieces, and the superiority of numbers in the proportion of five to four, and particularly of cavalry, in the proportion of three to one. Besides this inequality of force, two thirds of the troops under general Morgan were militia.

With these fair prospects of success lieutenant-colonel Tarleton, on the seventeenth of January 1781, engaged general Morgan, with the expectation of driving him out of the country. General Morgan had obtained early intelligence of Tarleton's force and advances, and drew up his men in two lines. The whole of the southern militia, with one hundred and ninety from North Carolina, under major McDowell, were put under the command of colonel Pickens. These formed the first line, and were advanced a few hundred yards before the second, with orders to form on the right of the second when forced to retire. The second line consisted of light-infantry, under lieutenant-colonel Howard, and a small corps of Virginia militia riflemen. Lieutenant-colonel Washington, with his cavalry, and about forty-five militiamen mounted and equipped with swords, under lieutenant-colonel McCall, were drawn up at some distance in the rear of the whole. The Americans were formed before the British appeared in sight. Lieutneant-colonel Tarleton halted and formed his men when at the distance of about two hundred and fifty yards from the front line of general Morgan's detachment. As soon as the British had formed they began to advance with a shout, and poured in an incessant fire of musketry. Colonel Pickens directed the militia under his command not to fire till the British were within forty or fifty yards. This order, though executed with great firmness and success, was not sufficient to repel the advancing foe. The

Americans were obliged to retire, but were soon rallied by their officers.

The British advanced rapidly and engaged the second line, which, after a most obstinate conflict, was compelled to retreat to the cavalry.* In this crisis of the battle lieutenant-colonel Washington made a successful charge upon lieutenant-colonel Tarleton who was cutting down the militia. Lieutenant-colonel Howard, almost at the same moment, rallied the continental troops, and charged with fixed bayonets. The example was instantly followed by the militia. Nothing could exceed the astonishment and confusion of the British, occasioned by these unexpected charges. Their advance fell back upon their rear, and communicated a panick to the whole. In this moment of confusion lieutenant-colonel Howard called to them to 'lay down their arms," and promised them good quarters. Upwards of five hundred accepted the offer, and surrendered. The first battalion of the seventy-first regiment, and two British light-infantry companies laid down their arms to the American militia. Previous to this general surrender, three hundred of the corps, commanded by lieutenant-colonel Tarleton, had been killed, wounded or taken. Eight hundred stand of arms, two field-pieces, and thirty-five baggage-waggons, also fell into the hands of the Americans. Lieutenant-colonel Washington pursued the British cavalry for several miles, but a great part of them escaped. The Americans had only twelve men killed and sixty wounded. General Morgan, whose great abilities were discovered by the judicious disposition of his force, and whose activity was conspicuous through every part of the action, obtained the universal applause of his countrymen. And there never was a commander better supported than he was by the officers and men of his detachment. The glory and importance of this action resounded from one end of the continent to the

---

* Perhaps Ramsay's grossest misstatement. As we have read elsewhere, the entire Continental line did not retreat, though a portion of its right flank did turn after misunderstanding an order. Howard quickly corrected the mistake, leading to the battle's decisive moment.

other. It re-animated the desponding friends of America, and seemed to be like a resurrection from the dead to the southern states.

General Morgan's good conduct on this memorable day was honoured by Congress with a gold medal. That illustrious assembly, on this occasion, presented also a medal of silver to colonel Washington, another to lieutenant-colonel Howard, a sword to colonel Pickens, a brevet majority to Edward Giles, the general's aide-de-camp, and a captaincy to baron Glasback, who had lately joined the light-infantry as a volunteer. This action reflected so much honour on the American arms, that general Morgan transmitted to Congress an official account of the names of the Continental officer who shared in the glory thereof. The British legion, hitherto triumphant in a variety of skirmishes, on this occasion lost their laurels, though they were supported by the seventh regiment, one battalion of the seventy-first, and two companies of light infantry. Lieutenant-colonel Tarleton had hitherto acquired distinguished reputation, but he was greatly indebted for his military fame to good fortune and accident. In all his previous engagements he either had the advantage of surprizing an incautious enemy—of attacking them when panic-struck after recent defeats—or of being opposed to undisciplined militia. He had gathered no laurels by hard fighting against an equal force. His repulse on this occasion did more essential injury to the British interest than was compensated by his victories.

Tarleton's defeat was the first link, in a grand chain of causes, which finally drew down ruin, both in North and South Carolina, on the royal interest.

Part Five: Congressional Proclamation and Related Correspondence

CHAPTER FIFTEEN:

CONGRESSIONAL PROCLAMATION AND RELATED CORRESPONDENCE*

Printed here is the proclamation by the Continental Congress awarding Daniel Morgan a gold medal for his heroics at Cowpens, making Morgan one of only seven American officers to receive this most prestigious of awards. The other six were: George Washington, Horatio Gates, Anthony Wayne, Nathanael Greene, Henry Lee, and John Paul Jones. Also recognized for their heroics at Cowpens in this proclamation were William Washington and John Eager Howard (silver medals), and Andrew Pickens (a presentation sword). But after the war, Congress struggled to meet its wartime obligations and debts, and also below is a letter from Morgan to his congressional representative, John F. Mercer, inquiring about the medal's manufacture and delivery. Finally, after a

---

* From *Cowpens Papers: Being Correspondence of General Morgan and the Prominent Actors*, Theodorus Bailey Myers, ed. (Charleston, SC: The News & Courier, 1881).

delay of nine years, Congress fulfilled its promise to Morgan, with George Washington's personal endorsement.

The Gratitude of Congress

Congress on Friday, March 9, 1781, recognized the value of this important victory as follows:

"The United States, in Congress assembled, considering it as a tribute due to distinguished merit to give a public approbation to the conduct of Brigadier General Morgan and of the officers and men under his command on the 17th of January last, when with eighty cavalry and two hundred and thirty-seven infantry of the troops of the United States and five hundred and fifty-three militia from the States of Virginia, North Carolina, South Carolina and Georgia he obtained a complete and important victory over a select and well appointed detachment of more than eleven hundred British Troops commanded by Lieut. Col. Tarleton, do therefore resolve,

"That the thanks of the United States in Congress assembled be given to Brigadier General Morgan and the men under his command for the fortitude and good conduct displayed in the action at the Cowpens, in the State of South Carolina, on the seventeenth day of January last: That a medal of gold be presented to Brigadier-General Morgan, a medal of silver to Lieutenant-Colonel Washington, of the Cavalry, and one of silver to Lieutenant-Colonel Howard, of the Infantry of the United States, severally, with emblems and mottoes descriptive of the conduct of those officers respectively on that memorable day.

"That a sword be presented to Colonel Pickens, of the Militia, in testimony of his spirited conduct in the action before mentioned.

"That Major Edward Giles, aid-de-camp to Brigadier-General Morgan, have the brevet commission of a Major; and that Baron de Glabuck, who served with

Brigadier-General Morgan as a Volunteer, have the brevet commission of a captain in the Army of the United States in consideration of their merit and services.

"Ordered that the commanding officers in the Southern Department communicate these resolutions general orders."

Daniel Morgan to General Lincoln and Hon. John F. Mercer,* February 6, 1783

DR. SIR—I am induced to trouble you with a few lines for two reasons. The first through a reliance on your friendship, which I flatter myself would prompt you to serve me if in your Power, and second because you are the only gentleman in office in Philadelphia whose acquaintance would countenance such a request.

The Honorable Congress after the action at Cowpens thought proper to vote me a Medal for my conduct in that affair, and as such an acknowledgement of my countrie's approbation could not but be flattering to the mind of a soldier I have made frequent application to get, and have been as frequently disappointed. Gen. Lincoln once informed me that nothing prevented its being sent to me but the low situation of finances, and I should have it as soon as there was money to be had to defray the Expense. Now sir, I not only wish you to expedite the making of it, but that you may also pay some attention to the manner in which it may be done, and with devices properly emblematical of the affair. I have so good an opinion of your taste and general knowledge as to wish to submit the matter entirely to your discretion, the expense cannot be considerable, and I flatter myself the Financier on a proper application would advance a sum sufficient to defray it, especially to gratify the inclinations of a

---

* John Francis Mercer was a Virginia delegate to the Continental Congress in 1783 and 1784.

man whose principal aim it has been to obtain his Country's applause to his conduct.

> I have the Honour, &c., &c., &c.,
>
> D. MORGAN.

George Washington to Daniel Morgan, March 25, 1790

Sir—You will receive with this a Medal struck by order of the late Congress in commemoration of your much approved conduct in the battle of Cowpens, and presented to you as a mark of the high sense which your Country entertains of your services on that occasion.

This Medal was put into my hands by Mr. Jefferson, and it is with singular pleasure that I now transmit it to you.

> I am Sir, with very great esteem, your most obedt servt,
>
> GEO. WASHINGTON

BATTLE OF COWPENS

ABOUT THE EDITOR

Andrew Waters is an author, editor, and conservationist. He is a graduate of UNC Chapel Hill (B.A. in English and Psychology) and UNC Greensboro (MBA), and is currently working on his Ph.D. in Parks & Conservation Area Management at Clemson University. He is the author of *The Quaker and the Gamecock: Nathanael Greene, Thomas Sumter, and the Revolutionary War for the Soul of the South* (Casemate), a study of the relationship of Nathanael Greene and Thomas Sumter during the American Revolution. He is also the editor of three slave narrative collections published by Blair: *Prayin' to Be Set Free* (Mississippi), *On Jordan's Stormy Banks* (Georgia), and *I Was Born in Slavery* (Texas). He currently resides in Spartanburg, South Carolina, with his wife, Anne, and son, Eli.

Andrew's books and articles can be found online at:
www.regimentpress.com

www.ingramcontent.com/pod-product-compliance
Lightning Source LLC
Chambersburg PA
CBHW021955290426
44108CB00012B/1083